The CEO: The Chief Engagement O̶f̶f̶i̶c̶e̶r̶

D0642273

The CEO: The Chief Engagement Officer

Turning Hierarchy Upside Down to Drive Performance

JOHN SMYTHE

GOWER

Published by
Gower Publishing Limited
Gower House
Croft Road
Aldershot
Hampshire
GU11 3HR
England

Gower Publishing Company
Suite 420
101 Cherry Street
Burlington
VT 05401-4405
USA

John Smythe has asserted his moral right under the Copyright, Designs and Patents Act, 1988, to be identified as the author of this work.

British Library Cataloguing in Publication Data
Smythe, John
    The CEO; chief engagement officer : turning hierarchy
    upside down to drive performance
    1. Employee motivation
    I. Title
    658.3'14

    ISBN-13: 9780566085611

Library of Congress Cataloging-in-Publication Data
Smythe, John.
    The CEO - chief engagement officer : turning hierarchy upside down to
    drive performance / by John Smythe.
        p. cm.
    Includes bibliographical references and index.
    ISBN 978-0-566-08561-1
    1. Communication in management. I. Title.
    HD30.3S578 2007
    658.4'5--dc22
                                                                2006100206

Printed and bound in Great Britain by MPG Books Ltd, Bodmin, Cornwall

Contents

List of Figures

List of Tables

Acknowledgements

This book has been incubating conceptually for about ten years, going back to when I was helping Kevin Hatton then MD of BA Cargo. In that programme lay the roots of the ideas which are expressed here. Kevin is a true first adopter. As is Patrick O'Sullivan who also experiments boldly with employee engagement. At the time of writing, he is at it again as Vice Chairman of Zurich Financial Services spearheading 'profitable growth'.

In that context I should also mention Matthew McCreight of management consultancy RHS&A, who taught me a lot about strategy execution and gave me insight about the role of employee engagement in driving execution.

In truth it is our clients who are taking the real risk of sharing power with their employees to drive value. I salute the risk takers one and all.

I also wish to acknowledge McKinsey and Company who, in 2004, asked me to join them as an organisational fellow for what turned into a ten month stint to carry out one of the biggest pieces of research into employee engagement on their and my own behalf.

Special thanks to Colin Price, Catherine Tilley, Nathalie Hourihan, Dominic Casserley, head of the London office, and of course Ian Davis, global head, who had long been interested in this aspect of change.

I should also mention all my former colleagues at SmytheDorwardLambert each of whose wisdom reflects in the book. In similar vein are many other special friends including competitors whose ideas have influenced me consciously and otherwise.

Lynette Proctor worked tirelessly on making it happen whilst attending to her day job of starting Engage for Change with Jerome Reback and I. Jerome's ideas are of course peppered throughout. Thanks are also due to Robert Nuttall at Marks and Spencer for helping with the McKinsey and Company research.

Thanks go to Johanna Fawkes for putting my ideas into a broader context in Chapter 12. Johanna was a Principal Lecturer at Leeds Metropolitan University until 2004. She led the BA in Public Relations and taught across the portfolio, specialising in mass communications and persuasive psychology. Her main areas of interest are public relations education and the role and ethics of persuasion in public relations theory and practice. She is a member of the Institute of Communication Ethics (ICE) Advisory Board and Chief Examiner for the Chartered Institute of Public Relations (CIPR) Diploma.

Thanks too go to Jonathan Norman from Gower, for his patience and quiet encouragement.

Most importantly thanks to my family; Fiona, Rosie and CoCo for putting up with me typing away on the weekends and holidays and keeping the whole show on the road! And finally thanks to our two rescued Brittany spaniels, Max and Alfie, who provided family therapy and fresh air throughout.

John Smythe

PART I

The End of Employee Coercion; The Beginning of Employee Engagement

1 The CEO: The Chief Engagement Officer: Leaders are Learning to Engage Their People to Drive Sustainable Performance and Change

Have you seen bosses come and go with their manifestos of change flying high one minute and forgotten the next?

Perhaps you are one of those bosses wondering how to engage hundreds or thousands of fellow colleagues in your vision, strategy or plans for your organisation. Maybe all you are sure of is that the organisation which you will temporarily lead has got to change its act.

Or perhaps you are one of the specialists in HR, communication or change who will be asked to 'align and mobilise' people with the change.

Either way my intention in this book is to:

- Put a spotlight on the current vogue for employee engagement.

- Ask what the concept means.

- Test whether it is different to internal communication and internal marketing or simply a repackaging of old ideas.

- Tell a few stories about how organisations are experimenting with engaging their employees to drive change and everyday performance, drawing from my temporary term as an Organisational Fellow with McKinsey and Company (where I researched into the phenomenon of employee engagement) and years of consulting in this arena.

- Propose a practical framework for those who want to engage their colleagues but need some advice based on practical experience.

- Reflect on the implications of engaging employees for leaders, internal advisers, sponsors of change and employees themselves, as their relationship in organisations changes from hired hands to citizens who have both rights and new responsibilities to take an active role in the governance of their organisations.

WHY WOULD YOU WANT ENGAGED EMPLOYEES?

In the course of the research into employee engagement conducted to inform this book, I interviewed many leaders and staff about the conditions and drivers which engaged them at work. All reported that being trusted with a stretching task within demanding timescales and a clear understanding of the discretion available to them brought the best out in them.

They said that engaged staff:

- are more creative and more productive;

- are constructively critical and challenging of the status quo and seek to initiate change;

- make other people's change their own;

- will advocate the company, not as robots or brand messengers, but from their own critical perspective;

- in short, enjoy their work and make it enjoyable for colleagues and external parties.

These sound like the sort of people we would all like to have working for us. But is it possible to create the conditions which stimulate these positive outcomes? In this book I hope to show that it is possible to do so. I also hope to address some of these questions:

- Does employee engagement actually result in people feeling good about their work and their organisation? Does it deliver retention of the right people?

- Most crucially, what are the specific causes or drivers of engagement?

- Are these causes or drivers generic to all workplaces?

- Can the causes or drivers of engagement be enhanced to increase engagement? In other words is it actionable?

- Is this enhancement ethical or does this 'social engineering' simply achieve greater performance through manipulation?

The concept of employee engagement is still highly fragmented and, as is clear from the final chapter (a review of recent studies of employee engagement by academic Johanna Fawkes), there is little academic underpinning as yet.

But as my research with McKinsey and Company showed – more of which later – there are many exciting experiments being undertaken by managers who sense and believe that the top-down model of decision making by the few imposed on the many must be augmented, if not replaced, by models which open up decision making to those who can add value.

I would venture that there is the beginning of a velvet revolution taking place in business with younger leaders and brave older ones saying: We bosses are no longer gods – who must have or pretend to have all the answers – but guides who need to govern who gets involved in decision making and creating a compelling place to work in the mutual interests of the business.

EMPLOYEE ENGAGEMENT MEANS OPENING UP DECISION MAKING AND CHANGE TO THOSE WHO WILL ADD VALUE, NOT FASTER MORE PERSUASIVE PROPAGANDA

With my temporary colleagues at McKinsey and Company we came to the conclusion that employee engagement is significantly driven by the degree to which people are usefully included in the decision-making process both day-to-day and in big-ticket change, crisis and transformation.

Thus it is about how power is shared and how that process is governed. Most employees no longer enjoy or subscribe to the old psychological contract in which security is exchanged for their compliance and loyalty. The old deal is dying because few employers can, or want, to offer the security end of the old deal. And they no longer want compliant people, they want people who will engage their creativity at work. Fat pensions are no longer deliverable and few employees want to work for the same employer for life.

They want employability and a say in their work and in how the business changes. They also only want to work for companies with ethics, values and a brand promise which they can at least sanction and, at best, approve of, even have affection for.

This book is mostly about giving employees a say in what will add value to the business and create an attractive and creative place to work

For me employee engagement is first and foremost a management philosophy based on the idea of including the right people in the right decisions at the right time in the right way. Inclusion in decision making and change is not a one-way ticket for employees to butt their noses in wherever and however they want. Leadership sets the boundaries and governs the process; and citizens in the process have responsibilities to behave as partners in the process.

Nor is employee engagement a free-for-all democracy or Marxism revisited; the prime outcome is to create more value by engaging the creativity of workers, an aim which will make the job better and thus bring benefits to workers too. Leaders and workers have to take risks to participate to avoid going back to bureaucratic relationships managed by go-betweens like unions and HR departments.

Nor is employee engagement about turbo-charged, more persuasive communication or internal marketing – though good communication can help to set the stage and equip people to participate – it is a management philosophy as this first story illustrates.

GLOBAL FREIGHT CARRIER STORY: WHAT EMPLOYEE ENGAGEMENT LOOKS LIKE

The first story of the book is about a global freight carrier which in the mid 1990s set out to reform years of rot. It was a part of a much larger global group and several CEOs had tried their hand at modernising the company. Back then it took an average of 6 days to get a piece of freight from A to B. As the latest incoming CEO of this unit said, he could cycle quicker on some routes!

Financial returns on some £700 million turnover was poor and had deteriorated so much that the main board had given the incoming CEO a year to show that the turnaround was possible or the unit would face outsourcing. The threat was real. The platform was ablaze, to borrow a phrase from John Kotter. The new CEO found that the error rate in delivering goods was appalling and worsening with each passing month. Customers were deserting to rival firms.

Still he reckoned that with his background in sales he could rally the troops around a cause.

How wrong he was. On arrival he found workers rest areas were no-go to management, employees pretty much decided rosters, people worked as little as 6 hours of an 8 hour shift. First-line management had been so let down by weak senior management they aligned themselves with those they were supposed to supervise and discipline. And discipline had broken down almost completely.

Theft was common. Manager's cars would acquire modifications of the undesirable kind in the car park. It was not a pretty sight!

Early attempts by the new CEO to galvanise the people via town halls were met with derision, cat calls and people showing their disdain by turning their backs.

Previous administrations had attempted process re-engineering, each of which had been suffocated by the breakdown in relationships between bosses and staff. The incoming CEO quickly realised that rational plans for re-engineering operations alone would not get off first base. He had to tackle the breakdown in relationships and in workplace discipline.

He also recognised that management was a core part of the problem. The unit was described as a 'Siberia posting' and many managers simply bided their time until they could get out. And whilst his team was anything but perfect he could not afford much more top-level churn. He had to show a united front. He got his team to sign up for a minimum period and worked with them to fashion a vision for the business which might compel others to fight for the business. It was important for people to see them coming together around a vision as much as it was to have a vision.

At the same time he instituted a back-to-basics programme on the shop floor, designed to wrest control of work rostering and day-to-day disciplines. At first this was very difficult. Workers tested the boundaries of their manager's resolve and soon it was clear that managers would need crowd-control techniques to impose discipline again. Managers learnt how to manage aggression, sullenness, heckling and dominant voices seeking to drown out those who ventured to cooperate.

So far this must sound like an example of a coercive management style. But it was imposed at the same time that daring inclusive initiatives were tested.

The CEO had surprised workforce and management alike with his determination and sense of purpose. They had not smelt a whiff of conviction like this for years. He surprised them again with a programme called 'The bad freight journey'. A real piece of freight was filmed in minute detail on a journey from Newark in North America to Verona in Italy via London's Gatwick airport. Along the way customers, staff, freight forwarders and other airport staff were interviewed seeking honest views as to why it took the freight company an average of 6 days to shift freight.

The lessons and insights were assembled into a half-day learning event in which the 6-day journey from Newark to Verona was presented in painstaking detail featuring 28 typical breakdowns. Every member of staff from around the world attended over 6 months. Word got back to those who had yet to attend the sessions that few managers or staff could put their hands up and say that they had no hand in one or more of the breakdowns. Gradually a collective acceptance crystallised: everyone was culpable for the mess; not just the blue collar and not just management, everyone.

Running in parallel was the most transparent communication process about the change process. The communication team always had a representative from the shop floor. These typically arrived cynical for their 3-month stint, but soon were to be found mucking in and even trying to persuade die-hard friends that this time the management seemed to have integrity of purpose, or in their language: 'they're not trying to stitch us up'.

Every month the CEO took 'the long walk' to the main board to report on progress. If all went well it would grant a £250 million investment to build a new facility, if not the whole operation would be outsourced. At first the staff used the opportunity to bet on the chances of the CEO making it back, but after a while they started to welcome his return.

As relations on the shop floor improved, the CEO brought back to life the process plans which had lain dormant. Work streams could now include widespread staff inclusion and unions were brought into the process.

An early decision was made to make it clear that whilst much about the change was negotiable, a staff cut of 25 per cent was not. At the same time shop-floor staff were asked to work on a futuristic experience to be built in an aircraft hanger which would allow staff to develop their own view of what working in the business could be like: 'Vision to Reality' was a huge set in which every aspect of the average freight journey was broken down into steps and job roles described and acted out for those visiting the experience. All the 'acting' performers were front-line staff from around the world, there were no managers 'on set'. Again high percentages of staff participated in Vision to Reality.

Vision to Reality made explicit to staff the nature of future jobs. It was a different world to the restrictive practices of the existing structures where staff working on 'imports' would not work on 'exports'. A ballot was called by unions about 9 months into the year before the board would decide the unit's fate, and much to everyone's surprise members voted to adopt the change plan by some 75 per cent. It was an outstanding result given that just 9 months or so previously, things looked and felt very grim. As a result the board granted the £250 million investment and the facility was built.

Some 8 years on there is still much to do and, as in any relationship, nothing stands still and the next generation of management is grappling with the next stages of modernisation.

This story has some powerful lessons and insights. The CEO recognised that more process plans would not work; nor would hero-style macho leadership. The people had dispatched a number of old style bosses. He knew that the relationships between management and staff would have to be tackled. He also knew that enough of the men and women on the line would have to decide for themselves that they wanted the business to survive. They had the power to subvert any instructional leadership.

Most of all he knew he would have to take risks: risks in ignoring calls to 'clamp down' and get on with it. Many of these were coming from a very old-style command-and-control parent company which had difficulty in understanding the point of including the workers in the ways I have summarised above. And risks from the unions that they would revert to old ways. In fact because they were included both at the national and local level much more than in the previous set up, they became very supportive and helpful.

The biggest risk that the CEO cited came from within himself: would he have the guts and stamina to stand alone on a different trajectory? Like most people who turn against accepted wisdoms he was, at first, a man alone. Yet as his conviction was sensed, he had many converts both in management and on the shop floor.

Together with this CEO we arrived at the capabilities that the chief engagement officer would have (regardless of whether they were a CEO or a call centre supervisor):

- advocate the company's vision;
- focuses people on the right work;
- pastoral care – knowing and delivering what engages their people;
- power sharing – considering who to engage in decision making and execution, and governing it well;
- authentic presence – having insight and exercising discipline about personal communication style and tone;
- attractive values – including fairness and transparency;
- (and is good at the day job).

Taking personal risk is a characteristic trait exhibited by all the leaders I interviewed about engagement. All were bucking either the system or, harder still, their own comfort zones about their natural preferences to engaging their people.

I hope this story has started to bring to life the concept of employee engagement. It is first and foremost a management philosophy and a real challenge to leadership.

CHALLENGES PRESENTED BY EMPLOYEE ENGAGEMENT

As I see it employee engagement presents three main challenges to organisations:

- the challenge to leadership;
- the challenge to the organisation's way of change;
- the challenge to the organisation's voice and way of communication.

Challenge to leadership

The challenge to leadership is to see employee engagement as a way of management or as a philosophy which influences the way managers and supervisors exercise a more inclusive style of decision making. Employees work in small spaces called teams and their world of work is largely dictated by the habits and beliefs of their manager or supervisor. They are the primary models of the culture and it is they who will live or belie good engagement practice.

Even in organisations where the espoused values echo the art of employee engagement, like Britain's John Lewis group, it may be that the ideals of inclusion are more evident in the rituals and architecture of formal decisions than on the line.

So living the philosophy of employee engagement also means considering how the principles of engagement influence the espoused and practised values and brand offer, particularly as the latter will be primarily experienced by clients and customers by interaction with the organisation's people.

It means thinking about how the role models who practice good engagement are reflected in the recruitment offer and development and learning processes.

Challenge to the organisation's way of change

Engagement may be a characteristic of day-to-day business life but then along comes change and all too often, and sometimes of necessity, the change juggernaut swings into action, smothering day-to-day values for the period of the crisis or change; a highly programmatic and instructional regime of decision making and execution sweeps all before it. The colonels have seized the state. It may that the organisation needs reform if not revolution.

But it is also true that change processes are often conducted as a matter of habit in the programmatic way, with a few taking all or most decisions, denying the organisation the wisdom of its people.

The challenge is to integrate these programmes with the principles and practices of employee engagement so that the value of the right people can be vested in the change and so that the employees own the end result rather than are afraid of it or sabotage it, which they can be expert at.

Challenge to the organisation's voice

You can read an organisation by listening to the metaphors in use. Many organisations, certainly in the Anglo Saxon world, are still reverberating with the metaphor of religion, the military and more recently marketing. All tend to suggest a hierarchic and instructional tone of voice where the plans and decisions of the few are conveyed to the masses via a battery, to use a military metaphor, of media, channels and face-to-face method designed to 'mobilise' and 'harness' people into some ordained plan.

The challenge to the organisation's voice lies in shifting from a coercive to an inclusive DNA. With the advent of new media and access to information, there can be no resisting this move. Employees loath and abhor the patronising, preachy, daddy-knows-best hectoring of many corporate cultures.

It is with this last challenge that I begin, not least because my experience of consulting has lain in the area of organisational communication and the communication role of leaders.

COMMUNICATION IN ORGANISATIONS HAS BECOME STUCK IN COMMAND AND CONTROL

A core argument of this book is that the employee communication movement which began in earnest in the 1980s has become stuck as a tool of the command-and-control style of leadership. The employee communication movement set out to balance the legitimate right of the employer to align its employees with its aims by creating workplace cultures which legitimised employees to challenge and influence.

In recent years that balance has swung almost completely to aligning people with the aims of the organisation. At the same time communication technology has multiplied and members of all organisations are bombarded with 'tell and sell' messages. As with any overuse of medication the impact has worn off and people are switching off.

The underlying discipline influencing the first era of employee communication was marketing. It is a flawed foundation for engaging employees as it casts employees as targets or customers to be persuaded and as human assets which the organisation feels it owns. I argue that individuals will engage more fully if they are invited to volunteer themselves in the organisation's success.

A whole internal/employee communication discipline comprising thousands of professionals working in consultancies and in corporations has grown up in the mass-marketing school of thought and with them the leaders of organisations have become used to using internal communication or internal marketing to get their messages, visions, strategies across using the tools of mass communication.

The underlying discipline which influences the practice of employee communication needs to shift from mass marketing to individual and collective learning. Learning in organisations has been confined to developing skills and knowledge. Now its role should extend to the way leaders and employees understand and engage in the need for change in both the big picture and at their place of work. Such a shift will require a complete rewrite of the way organisations communicate and engage with leaders and employees.

Marketing; a flawed foundation for engaging employees

Internal communication was born as a late sibling to external marketing and the language of internal communication is still rich with the echoes of military and religious metaphor: capturing hearts and minds, conversion, mobilisation, indoctrinate the troops, team brief, feedback from the front line, cascading the belief system, engaging, inculcating vision and values and so on. As such the marketing philosophy is essentially coercive, top down – a tool of the command-and-control leadership style.

In the 1980s and 1990s the putative discipline of internal communication borrowed the instincts of marketing and within a few years turned employees into 'internal customers' who were marketed at as any other 'stakeholder group' when plans were drawn up to refresh the company's strategy or its products and services.

Internal communication was born in the fag-end of the command-and-control era of leadership. The brains were thought to be at the top of the organisation and decisions and values were cascaded from the mighty few to the many. The role of organisational communication was to align the many with the few. Communication was essentially a process of crafting the messages of the few and ensuring their propagation and replication.

It was Soviet in its aim to control the dialogue and voice of the people.

Companies became good at the 'sheep-dip' style of giving everyone the same script. A whole industry has arisen in which designers, communicators and behavioural/training/event specialists collude to get everyone 'singing off the

same song sheet', choreographing the customer experience in such a way that what they see, hear and experience is similar.

But the success of internal communication in this idiom bore with it the seeds of its demise. Constant testing of employee satisfaction has raised expectations of 'being satisfied' at work. At the

Source: Istockphoto/Roberta Casaliggi

same time relentless internal marketing about the next change/product/brand initiative means that employees are saturated with data and then researched to death to see if they're satisfied.

They are not. Why not? Because they have less and less control and less and less say. And as in any relationship where one side routinely controls the agenda, the other gives up overt resistance, assumes an outward face of compliance and puts in the minimum effort.

I argue that the marketing philosophy of internal communication is one cause of driving energy out of individuals at work. The good intent to inform often suffocates or simply bores people into switching off. Bosses are often bemused to find that when they reach the top the power they thought would attend them is elusive. Rank receives much less admiration than in times when people could not escape the hierarchy.

Take the case of the investment bank CEO who constantly bombarded staff with a systematic programme of voice, text and town hall meetings, following the advice that to get through the noise, leaders had to be the dominant voice. For a while it worked; people said we have a leader with conviction.

But soon enough people wearied of the constant barrage of exhortation and the number of unread and unlistened-to messages spiralled. People showed up to town halls but more to show face than to engage. The same bank began to lose key teams, not because the pay was better down the street but because the managing directors and team leaders adopted the tell mode of decision making. They left because they sought a more egalitarian environment in which their voice would be welcomed in day-to-day decision making and change.

The CEO was baffled because he thought he was spending time communicating, following advice that this meant being a demigod. His moment of insight occurred when seated at the head of his 20-strong team of managing directors: he asserted in the strongest terms that everyone knew the strategy because he had briefed and communicated about it exhaustively. It was true he had. Yet when I asked the group to privately write down their understanding of the strategy each had a different take. They had been told many times but they had since stopped listening because they had not been invited to engage and contribute.

PHILOSOPHY UNDERPINNING INTERNAL COMMUNICATION MUST CHANGE

Employees are unhappy, dissatisfied and depressed despite, and maybe because of, the sophisticated attempts to 'customise' and communicate at them: because seeing them as customers has made them targets for persuasion. And given that employees are increasingly making join and stay decisions on their perceptions of an organisations' real belief and value systems, organisations which treat them as targets to be aligned and marketed to, no longer appeals.

Today, what people want from work is the space and licence to think things through for themselves and add a little bit of their own creativity and their own insight to their daily work, to the new brand, the customer experience and to the continuous change and major transformation processes.

But this is not what they get. The predominant engagement practice is for top management or elite teams to make all the decisions and then to mobilise engagement and support amongst the troops using the internal communication processes and infrastructures and campaigns involving events and sheep-dip training to inculcate the new.

Management teams say that they want people to feel involved, by which they mean they want their message sugar coated. Streetwise employees cringe when they hear bosses say they want people to feel involved. This is code for 'we've decided what's best for you but we want to manipulate you into thinking that you were part of the decision making'. This is the commercial equivalent of government running a few focus groups and spinning the results to justify doctrinaire legislation.

It rarely means actually involving people in the decision making and implementation.

It is worth pausing to look back at the dozens of velvet revolutions from Eastern Europe, Africa, South America and others brewing in the Middle East. In doing so we realise that we are witnesses to a great period of liberalism on the stage of nations. Not all have gone smoothly and reversals are inevitable.

Yet when we look at the internal cultures of many, if not most, corporations and institutions we find intolerant regimes that attempt to control internal media, dictate scripts and behaviours which employees must use to 'project the brand', marginalise protesters who challenge the status quo and attempt social engineering on a grand scale under the ironic banners of 'people development' or 'brand alignment'.

Many of us have probably worked for institutions which more closely resemble former small Soviet republics than models of liberal capitalism.

Of course there is much well-intentioned effort to create an orderly and consistent response to the outside world by companies and public institutions. Finding the right place on a continuum from ill-disciplined chaos at one extreme, in the centre a consistent brand based in a healthy, creative culture, to a corporate rule-bound strait jacket at the other extreme, is a tough challenge.

But creating a workplace culture which encourages people to participate and contribute is a core role for leaders and for the CEO. The CEO must truly become the Chief Engagement Officer.

Compliance vs personal engagement

Such is the grip of this marketing-based philosophy that organisations now defend it as the modern way of engaging people. And yet the results are wearisome compliance with the status quo by nearly everyone including top management.

Real engagement is based on the idea that people are more animated, creative and positive if they feel they are able to think things through for themselves and are able to add a little creativity of their own as opposed to learning by rote and complying with passed-down philosophy, practice and instructions.

In practice real engagement means asking people to think the business issue through for themselves and to have had insight about their place and possible contribution to the programme, whether it be change, transformation, strategy or everyday delivery.

IS EMPLOYEE COMMUNICATION A NEW PHENOMENON?

No, of course not.

Nelson didn't call his way of leadership 'employee engagement' or use the present day military term 'mission command' but he was an early advocate of engagement at least as far as his ships' captains went. He discussed and agreed objectives with them but left it to them to take the initiative and interpret the objectives as battles unfolded. His French opposite number Villeneuve was an advocate of command-and-control: his captains had to follow instructions to the letter, or I should say flag signals – the BlackBerry of the day!

Nelson also intuitively understood that personal style was a part of engaging his men in the task to hand. All his biographers note his mixture of discipline tempered with a tremendous empathy, not to mention a flair for the theatrical. In the confined social ecosystem of the British Navy of the nineteenth century, Nelson added value to the business of defeating his European enemies by engaging his staff in the decision making, not by dictating his vision and strategy at them.

15

A little later on in the twentieth century, workers experienced various movements designed to swing the balance of power more fairly in their favour. The union movement must take first credits but so too must the Japanese for the quality movement, later adopted by the Americans and British with particular enthusiasm. Others include the employee relations movement which marked the transition of the old personnel function from pay, benefits and discipline to people development.

In the 1990s 'empowerment' made a colourful appearance and was much paraded by corporations as a way to drive performance. Confusion often ensued because the rhetoric was usually in contrast to behaviour and practices. In short the time was not yet ripe to challenge the almost feudal central power of the corporations and empowerment passed as a fad.

In the 1990s people were still more or less owned by the company. They were still willing to trade their loyalty and compliance for security of tenure and a guaranteed pension. But with the demise of the latter and the rise of the portfolio career, organisations no longer owned human assets but borrowed talent for as long as people found value in staying with their employer.

Today people want three main things, aside from money, from their employer:

- employability to grow or go;

- opportunities to participate in decisions which affect them or to which they can add value;

- ethics and values they identify with.

This book explores the second of these employee drivers: finding the right balance between, at one extreme, the autocratic handing down of decisions, strategy and solutions from on high and, on the other, creating an ill-disciplined environment where over-empowerment results in confusion.

The key is making the right judgement about how much space to give people in order to address the organisational issue to hand, be it a change to product or service, a culture or brand repositioning, a change or transformation programme.

So whilst there is nothing new about the concept of employee engagement the times have changed particularly with the demise of the psychological contract which wedded employees to their company. Add to this the mobility of labour across national boundaries and the coming digital revolution in the workplace which will make engaging huge numbers of people in decision making irresistible and inevitable, the time is ripe for business leaders to reflect on how they engage their people to add value and create a compelling place to work.

For those readers who think this is all about a Marxist perspective, let me reassure you that I believe employee engagement is anything but an open-toed sandal, hippy, socialist agenda.

I contend that it will certainly create a much more attractive and compelling place to work, but as well as that it will help bring the wisdom, knowledge and experience of the people to the table. Leaders who learn to engage their people will be giving themselves a fantastic lead over their rivals who are still trying to do it all themselves.

Leadership will become 'leadership lite'. The burden will be shared by implicating those who can and want to make it happen, even where this involves very hard and unpopular decisions such as cost reduction and closures.

Those who have most to gain are societies where regulation does not govern or influence every interaction between employer and employee. The employers who voluntarily take the risk of sharing power by engaging their people will have a great advantage over rivals who have to abide by, or choose to hide behind, bureaucratic workplace regulation.

The European Union is progressive in respect of opening up markets but meddlesome and wrong to regulate the way corporations engage their people. By doing so the EU reinforces polarised relations between companies and employees and has helped to extend the life of command and control, hierarchical styles of corporate leadership so beloved of old Europe.

The Asians and East Europeans should beware of importing this level of state interference into the workplace and instead ensure that the principles of engaging workers to drive performance is at the heart of new models of popular liberal capitalism.

RIGHT LEVEL OF ENGAGEMENT – ENTIRELY DEPENDENT ON THE BUSINESS SITUATION TO HAND

This well-known, much-copied and outdated Smythe Dorward Lambert diagram devised in 1989 (Figure 1.1) illustrated the choice which leaders needed to make when deciding if, and how, to engage people in a decision or change process.

There will be plenty of situations where the business situation demands an instructional approach. But there will be others where the change is more adaptive, where instruction leads to resistance and even sabotage.

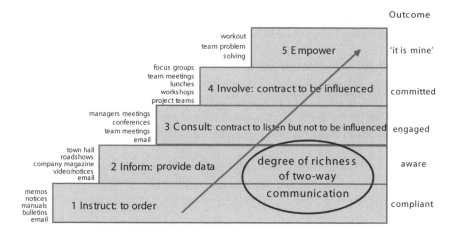

Source: Smythe Dorward Lambert

Figure 1.1   Leaders' choices when engaging people

The right approach to engaging employees in order to derive benefits for the business, is to focus on the desired outcomes of engaging people in the project (be it a change to product, service, culture, brand or an organisational change/transformation) as part of the up-front conceptual design. Usually engagement of management and employees is the last item on the agenda and the last box on the critical path.

Factoring it in earlier means thinking through:

- Which groups or individuals will add value if they are invited to be involved in the design of the project at the right time, both to the 'big idea' and to the way it is implemented?

- Whatever the degree of engagement in devising the change, what should both the *rational* and *emotional* experience of implementation of the change be like for those on the receiving end? Should it be the way 'we typically roll out change around here'? Does the typical way of change turn people on or off? Do we know?

- What therefore should the *rational* and *emotional* engagement process be like so that it turns people on rather than off? What activities and what style of activity will turn people on to achieve the desired business outcomes of the change or transformation?

By factoring the question 'should we engage our people?' earlier in the decision-making/project design process we force ourselves to consider the benefits, risks and costs of engaging (or not) as an integral part of the way leadership develops the change/product/brand/strategy/vision/transformation plan.

By leaving it to the end of the business planning or design process, leadership almost certainly casts the engagement process into a 'tell' programme which, for most organisations, is the default.

Contrastingly the purpose of real engagement is to put people at the heart of the change and decision-making process to make change faster and more sustainable.

EMPLOYEE EXPERIENCE BECOMES CUSTOMER EXPERIENCE

A further insight from the broad-scale research into employee engagement, which I conducted whilst acting as a visiting fellow with McKinsey and Company, is that external customers experience reduced service levels when employees are neutralised by programmatic, often brutal change.

It's no good organisations saying 'we haven't the time to engage people properly'. The employees are on the journey of the change and that journey is their experience of the promised land. The journey of implementation of change shapes their attitudes and outward behaviour much more than any values or brand promise. That means thinking about and influencing the engagement journey which employees will experience, as much as the arrival point. This is not to argue against the need for tough action. There are often times when tough action is required. But it is to argue for rational consideration of who will add value to a decision before it is complete both to improve the quality of the decision and to build support for it.

I will finish this chapter by returning to the topic of employee communication with a short history.

BRIEF HISTORY OF INTERNAL COMMUNICATION

From an organisational perspective it's a short history; for while every leader has been practising the art of good communication with their followers since we emerged as a species, its emergence as an organisational activity is more recent.

The Second World War is a reasonable place to start. Hitler had turned the weapon of propaganda onto the British people. Churchill responded with rhetoric, a style which is still emulated today. The Second World War was as much one of winning hearts and minds as it was of military exchanges.

Shortly after the end of the war in 1948 the Government information service was born. Its purpose was to communicate the policies of the government of the day in a non-partisan way. The press office was born. It represented the first tentative steps towards more open government – a recognition that governments must account for themselves.

Commanding and Controlling

Commercial organisations copied the public sector and hired journalists to represent themselves first externally and then internally. Channels like the house newspaper were born and so was internal communication. It wasn't long before employees routinely referred to their company news channels as *Pravda,* the name of the house newspaper of the old Soviet Union's communist party machine which contained what the state wanted its people to hear about.

Other early company channels were like community journals. Much was made of births, marriages, deaths, sports and social, merit awards and the like. Over time they became more business focused and, as the spirit of marketing took hold of internal communication, journals and all the other media have become tools of persuasion and in many cases crude coercion.

Today the credibility of much internal media in the eyes of staff is questioned.

Management have taken over 'the radio station' and mostly use it to spin their own story. Until recently this was seen as entirely legitimate. Many a manager would admit to thinking, if not saying, that during work time the company owns their people and has the right to influence them in line with achieving commercial aims. Up to a point this is valid. But it ignores the breakdown in loyalty of employees brought about by the erosion of the cradle-to-grave concept of employment, the destruction of adequate company pensions and the rise of the multi-company career.

Companies may think they have captive employees but employees have other ideas. American writer John Kotter tells us that in his research of employees going through change, they barely listen to any corporate messages at all – much noise, little impact.

In short it's time to change the way organisations manage communication with their people. It's time to move from a tell 'em, sell 'em approach based on a marketing idiom to an approach based on intelligent inclusion.

Much is being said about engaging employees. In this book I hope to throw some light on what is meant by the idea of engaging people and what it means for leadership style, how organisations communicate with their people and how they build more inclusive approaches into day-to-day decision making and change and strategy formulation and execution. It is based on my experience as a practitioner over many years first serving within three American corporations in corporate communication, then as co-founder of Smythe Dorward Lambert, a UK-based organisational communication consulting firm and now as a co-founder of Engage for Change, a consultancy which advises corporations on how best to engage their people.

Additionally I had the good fortune to be invited by McKinsey and Company to join them in a temporary capacity as an Organisational Fellow, a sort of visiting partner. Over 10 months in 2004 I undertook a piece of research into engaging leaders and everyone at work in change. It served to confirm my hypothesis that the command-and-control style of developing and executing strategy, change and everyday performance was beginning to give way to more inclusive approaches. The book draws heavily from the interviews I did in 59 organisations at various levels supported by my friend Robert Nuttall (now Director of Internal Communication at British high street retailer Marks & Spencer) and business partner Jerome Reback.

In my McKinsey and Company research study into engagement practices of large organisations, 'Boot Camp or Commune?', business leaders concluded that well-governed engagement matters to business leaders for a variety of reasons:

- If the right groups are engaged they will add value to day-to-day decisions and larger processes of change.

- The style of engagement adopted by leaders will turn people on or off.

- Positive engagement practices could pre-empt reliance on bureaucratic consultation processes imposed by regulation.

- Customers may benefit.

- Decisions are not complete until leaders have planned the engagement of their people.

The book concludes with a chapter written by academic Johanna Fawkes on other sources of views about employee engagement and therefore acts as a possible springboard for those who want to explore the topic further.

2 What Engaging People Means

To form a view about what employee engagement is and how it comes about I ask you first to transport yourself into the shoes of a mid-level employee in your organisation and reflect on the typical experience they have of being communicated to, and engaged with, by their boss and the organisation.

What would characterise the day-to-day experience of being communicated with by their immediate boss? How encouraging might this be? What involvement in decision making might be extended? How good an emissary of the organisation's brand and values are they? Do they take people into their confidence? Are they inspiring and confidence building? Do they take an interest in setting the mood by doing simple things like noticing people, saying good morning and congratulating people on good work and constructively criticising when appropriate?

And what is the experience of organizational communication? Do they get the inside track on big developments before the outside world? Do they feel they are treated as a member of a community which is trusted? Can they influence and contribute to the development of the company? Can they challenge and debate with immediate and distant leaders in safety?

When there is change, is the nearest thing they get to involvement in the change a briefing or indirect communication? Do they feel like spectators at someone else's party or victims of a machine?

Let's remember that people work in small spaces in the organisation. For most employees, communication and engagement lies in the gift of the local manager or supervisor; other organisational communication is usually clinically delivered in print and electronically or received via ritualistic processes like face-to-face meetings, conferences, town halls and electronic gatherings.

Jot down the kinds of words that might be used by the occupants of the shoes I asked you slip into for a few moments and reflect on whether that person is likely to feel incited to engage fully in pursuit of the company's interests?

It's time for an ice cream! Well an imaginary one anyway.

Source: Istockphoto/
Todd Harrison

ICE CREAM EXERCISE: WHAT DOES ENGAGEMENT TASTE LIKE?

To come to your own view about what engagement means I would now like to invite you to fill your own shoes and reflect on the last time that you were really engaged in a project at work by way of the ice cream exercise. What was the project? What made it special and rewarding for you and the company? Can you recall the conditions or drivers which brought about your engagement?

In organisations I ask people to do the ice cream exercise in pairs, each telling the other their story. Stressed executives quickly unwind over a favourite memory rather as they might over a children's story and when asked what good engagement looked like they report that they felt trusted by the sponsoring party to take on a challenge which they never imagined they would be considered for.

Sometimes people have to go back to a previous organisation or years back to recall a powerful story of their own engagement. When they do their eyes light up and taut faces relax with a reminder of the confidence that they recalled feeling in themselves at the time. People smile and tell their stories animatedly.

We know that the most engaged are the self-employed, bosses, artisans working their own agenda, people in self-directed work teams, people with bosses who know when to push and when to let people get on with it, taxi drivers, train drivers and pilots. In short it is people who feel they have a reasonable degree of influence over their work and indeed their lives. Much of this thinking can be applied to life outside work including relationships. The least engaged are those who have lesser influence on their work, lives and relationships.

In relationships, in work or at home, it is easy for all of us to blame the other party when things are not going well. In relationships it is incumbent on each of us to engage to get what we need and give what is necessary for the other party. That means taking risks with what we think and feel. It means being willing to see things with the eyes of the other party.

At work it is not just up to the boss or supervisor to engage their people in the decision making. As employees or workers we also need to take risks by participating and using our creativity and ideas. It is a two-way trade with both parties taking risks to cross the unstated boundaries which normally define who takes and who contributes to decisions. But it is undoubtedly the boss, the party with power, who must set the stage to make it safe for workers to risk taking the initiative or contributing their ideas. Most have memories or myths of the last time so-and-so stuck their neck out and got their head shot off!

Let's return to the ice cream exercise. Many stories from players come to mind. Here are some. A truck driver working for a big logistics company was tasked with evaluating the next model of truck for the fleet. It's a huge responsibility, one which will impact the efficiency, profitability and reputation of the company for many years and normally a decision taken by a few top managers. Charged with evaluating the options the storyteller and his group set out by creating a score card of stakeholders which the winning truck had to satisfy. Worried managers who thought the truckers would be overly swayed by looks, comfort and other hygiene factors need not have worried. The truckers group became tougher than any team populated by accountants and procurement because they did the job and asked questions which only a driver would think to ask.

Another told the story of being tasked with developing a counter-attack to a surprise entry by a new competitor into their niche market. The situation required unheard-of collaboration across many silos which had previously been impervious to each other. Her face became luminous at the memory of being at the epicentre.

A quiet women told an amazing story of being involved in skippering a boat in the Fastnet race, a major long-haul sailing event from the Isle of Wight, off the southern English coast, to the Fastnet rock in the Irish Sea off Ireland's stormy south-east tip. Her colleagues gasped as they had no previous knowledge of this individual's untapped resolve and potential team leadership, so far undeveloped at work.

In discussing the drivers or conditions which are conducive to bringing about their own engagement, participants in the ice cream exercise use words and phrases like these:

- shocked to be invited to participate in such a key exercise;
- surprised at the level of creativity used by the company to set the stage for our involvement;
- trusted with something normally given to more experienced or senior people;
- stretched way beyond my normal comfort zone;

- into the unknown;

- made totally accountable;

- given the right amount of time, but not too much;

- saw the difference it made to the end result;

- blank piece of paper;

- an authentic invitation to influence decision making rather than a management exercise in 'making the staff feel involved' (a sentiment that employees feel patronised by and one which dumbs employees down).

In these exercises pennies drop, light bulbs go on. Within a short space of time most executives can see that to engage their own and their people's interest and creativity means giving them ownership of a challenging task or project and making them accountable for proposing solutions. I expect if you have recalled a past or current project which has truly engaged you it will also be characterised by these or similar drivers or conditions.

I then ask the participants to recall the kinds of processes which they or their company normally employ in an effort to engage staff. To do so I ask:

What key words and phrases come to mind when executives are keen to engage or communicate with employees? Perhaps you too might jot down what words you and staff might use to characterise engagement or communication associated with your own leadership style and that of the organisation. It might help to recall a recent change process and the language used in the planning sessions when it came to 'getting our people on board'.

As I mentioned in the first chapter, military and religious metaphors like these abound:

- campaign;

- tell them, tell them what you have told them, and tell them again;

- capture hearts and minds;

- align staff with the strategy;

- brief;

- cascade the message;

- enrol and recruit;

- get them onside;

- convert;

- crush the opposition;

- get them singing off the same song sheet;

- get on the programme or get off the bus;

- convert into brand ambassadors;

- front-line.

If these words and phrases and others like them are the lingua franca of your own engagement and communication activities you may reasonably conclude that your employees do not enjoy the conditions which will encourage their engagement with your aims and ambitions. You may even still be under the impression that instructional communication is a symbol of strong leadership, that people will appreciate being told what to do because staff don't want to have to think for themselves.

The evidence from my extensive research is otherwise. It is only those who are used to a rigid command-and-control style of leadership who may express comfort with continuity of this approach to telling people what to do. They have become accustomed and simply don't know how to operate in apparent uncertainty.

Most employees want to contribute their creativity to their work and to the greater good of their organisation. The story behind staff turnover figures is that employees leave their bosses not their companies. And one of the biggest triggers is being excluded from contributing to day-to-day decision making which affects their jobs and in times of change to major change.

Employees put much of this down to insecurity by bosses who are nervous of looking weak by asking for help; bosses who hate to admit they don't know the answers; bosses who won't go on stage until they have been briefed with a prescribed line; or bosses who are unwilling to share power. Many bosses simply don't understand what engaging their employees means and involves. Many assume that it means deploying more engaging or entertaining communication; giving employees information and making them feel involved.

WHAT DOES ENGAGEMENT REALLY MEAN?

In the McKinsey and Company research we concluded that engagement is a process by which people become personally implicated in the success of a strategy, change, transformation or everyday operational decision. To become personally implicated, people want to contribute to everyday decision making in their place of work and to bigger change or transformation affecting the organisation and ultimately their work.

As a result of becoming personally implicated, people commit themselves with the fervour normally reserved for business start-ups, hobbies and relationships, the kind of fervour which is evident in the ice cream exercise when people recall a project which liberated their creativity.

What gets them to become personally implicated? Have another look at the list above of what engages people. Or better still recall what engages you personally.

People engage when they are trusted and given clearly defined discretion to get on with a task or project, when they have to find solutions for themselves and when they are made accountable for an end result which adds value.

In these situations bosses have shared power and involved people in decision forming, having taken the view that they will get a better result by opening up the decision to others who may know more or different things to them, or be in a position to provide an alternative approach which challenges the status quo. (See Figure 2.1.)

ENGAGING EMPLOYEES AND WORKERS INVOLVES LEADERS AND SUPERVISORS IN SHARING POWER

Creating an engaged group therefore means that bosses need to consider who will add value if they include them in decision forming and be willing to share power to those they engage. It also means managing the process of engagement by creating conditions in which people feel safe and legitimised

Power sharing

Rational consideration of who should be included in decision/change to create most value for the organisation and a climate of creative challenge for its citizens.

A personal process (not a marketing process)

A well-designed social process by which people become personally implicated in the success of a strategy, change, transformation or everyday operational improvement.

Source: John Smythe and McKinsey & Company

Figure 2.1   Requisites for engagement

to take the power offered and respect it. The right conditions for people means:

- a personal and collective journey of self discovery resulting in personal insight about:
    - the broader organisational change or day-to-day decisions;
    - how these affect their own work;
    - their own attitudes, values and skills.
- a process over which people feel some influence rather than just being a spectator of a top-down decision or programmatic change programme.

Think about that favourite project or positive situations away from work where you are really focused. It might be a hobby, a charity or community activity, a study programme or a family activity. In these situations people choose to volunteer themselves. We perform our own needs analysis and we feel we have sufficient influence over the process. We certainly do not feel like a spectator or a victim.

It could be a negative situation, say for example a relationship breakdown or exclusion from a favourite activity. Either way our relationship with the activity is intensely personal and emotional. So too at work, there will be little rational intellectual engagement until people have emotionally volunteered themselves to the cause or project. This requirement speaks volumes for the way leaders and supervisors need to set the stage for engaging their colleagues and for the way that change programmes are designed.

Positive engagement is marked by creative energy and personal ownership. Poor engagement is characterised by fear, fatigue and distrust. In these situations we rarely feel we have much influence. Awareness of the balance of power is key. In any relationship where we can elect to stay or go, if one party continually overpowers the other, the overpowered will be neutralised, withdraw, sabotage or fight.

How personally implicated are we in a change or strategy process? I would say that most people's relationship with change at work is negative. It is about mitigating loss or running to catch up with it. It rarely exhibits the attributes of positive engagement. Why is this so? From my research I believe it is because in organisational change most of us feel done to. We feel like spectators or even victims at someone else's programme.

We respond with fear, fatigue and distrust; attributes hardly likely to create the levels of personal implication organisations need. Think again of that relationship we have been in where we always see the other party as taking charge or manipulating us to give a false feeling of being involved in the decision making.

What is the relevance of all this at work?

I see engagement as a practical capability which leaders, at every level in an organisation, can develop and utilise to invite their people to bring the best out in themselves for their own benefit and for that of their colleagues and the company. Leaders, managers and supervisors are the lead component of the day-to-day culture of the workplace. They decide if and by how much to involve others in decisions large and small.

Managers and supervisors are the chief engagement officer in their own domain. Thus in creating an engaging workplace the main lever has to be the leaders, managers and supervisors.

A NARROW DEFINITION OF EMPLOYEE ENGAGEMENT

I see employee engagement as being about the role and influence people have been given in everyday decision making and in broader organisational change and strategy. I see it as being a practical capability which can be developed by leaders at every level to help them create value for the organisation by engaging the right people in decision forming and by so doing creating an attractive workplace experience where people can influence and feel ownership.

I define employee engagement narrowly as an integral part of decision making, as distinct from broader definitions arguing that involvement in decision making is no longer an occasional concession but a necessity for bosses to release the wisdom and experience of their people.

Most definitions are more systemic concepts in which the employee is said to be engaged when a whole variety of drivers are lined up like pay, conditions, values, the boss's behaviour, job content and so on. In Chapter 6 I look at these broader concepts of employee engagement and try to identify a narrower range of significant drivers of employee engagement and argue that trying to manage or create a culture by trying to fix all the supposed drivers is a grandiose vanity of bloated corporate functions.

These efforts are usually marked by the presence of large-scale 'engagement surveys' which attempt to measure every alleged source of employee engagement, whilst most are little more than rebranded employee satisfaction surveys. Hands up who still hankers after 'satisfied' employees? In Chapter 6 I do my best to debunk them as a measure of workplace culture which are past their sell-by date and a lead indicator of a failing organisation.

In my experience they only add value when care is taken to first identify drivers of business performance which are unique to each organisation and subsequently to draw some modest conclusions about how managers and supervisor's engagement practices contribute to high or low business performance. And that means making employee engagement personal for each and every manager and supervisor. Grand surveys painting systemic patterns of satisfaction give managers who want to create a local climate of creative contribution little specific help.

I am of the view that broad concepts of employee engagement are of little practical use to managers and leaders. In my view employee engagement is largely an outcome of the routine engagement practices of bosses at every level. That the place to look is into the small spaces and teams where people work. None of us work for the mighty corporation. Day-to-day we work for Doris and Gianni, our managers and supervisors. It is their engagement practices, their approach to power and command that shapes our opportunity to contribute and their mood which dictates whether we will risk engaging and contributing.

Therefore in trying to define employee engagement I have focused first on the leader's capacity to engage in ways which add value to everyday decision making and change. But I also contend that the way organisations design and open up broad-scale change to the right groups is critical to adding value. I attempt to provide some very down-to-earth advice on both the leader's/ supervisor's role in employee engagement and the design and running of creative and practical engagement interventions as part of change and transformation in later chapters.

Making employee engagement personal means seeing it from the perspective of both the leader and the employee. Both have a different perspective:

- The leader's dilemma – every decision large or small involves a leader (a CEO, a manager or a supervisor) deciding who to involve in forming the decision (or in contributing to the strategy or change) while balancing the tension between the apparent speed of a directive approach against the potential of added value and sustainability of a greater degree of inclusiveness.

- The employee experience – for leaders and employees who need to be engaged to bring about the change or executive decision, engagement can be defined as successful by the degree to which participants:

  - identify with the need or opportunity for change;

  - own and feel responsibility for their part in making it happen;

  - are disposed to discretionary action;

  - have insight about the need or opportunity for personal change and growth in the context of the change;

  - can see how all the elements of change/strategy fit together.

Too often employee engagement is discussed as an end in its own right and attendant programmes designed to improve engagement are done without so much as a nod to the organisation's reason for existence; its customers or clients.

Since the original 1998 Sears research, reported in the Harvard Business Review (Rucci, A. J., Kirn, S. P., Quinn, R. T. (2000), 'The Employee-Customer-Profit Chain at Sears'), there have been other studies demonstrating the link between the employee experience and customer satisfaction.

Thus I stress the need to develop a view about key drivers of employee engagement by taking into account internal and external stakeholders, especially customers and clients. Employees will also relate to a focus on engagement if it is done with a view to making the customer experience a more productive and distinctive one.

Figure 2.2 is a representation of the categories of key drivers (or influences) on attitudes, sentiments and behaviours which influence employees and customers. Approaches to identifying and tracking these are discussed in Chapter 6.

TURBO-CHARGED PRESENTATION OR CONSIDERED POWER SHARING?

It is worth making a distinction between communication and engagement.

As one CEO put it to me, communication is essential to set the context for engagement and to provide people with a sense of journey. Other CEOs

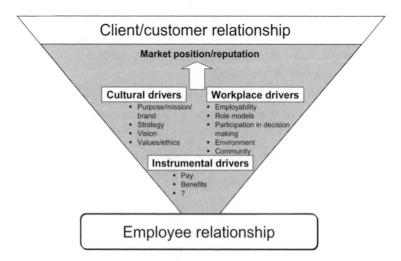

Figure 2.2   **Drivers to deliver a distinct customer offer and a compelling place to work**

mentioned that engagement meant consciously considering who would add value to the outcome of a change or decision if they were enfranchised early in the process. They recognised that engagement also means considering who should have influence over the decision.

While researching how organisations engage their people, I was struck how unclear people were about the concept of engagement. CEOs and others only clarified their concepts when I asked them to tell me the story of a recent change and how they had engaged their people in the process. To most the telling of the story revealed how little they considered the process of engagement as a part of designing the change or strategy. It got delegated to others and usually repeated past patterns of engagement. It was invariably an impulsive, irrational act.

At this point it might be valuable for readers to consider their own definition of engagement and when back at work ask colleagues to write and subsequently compare these. Without a robust and shared definition, preparing an approach to engagement will be confusing.

I attempt to summarise the difference between communication and engagement in Figure 2.3.

I must add a few words about the pandemic use of phrases like 'what are the messages we want people to get?'. I always cringe when I hear myself or others say this because the sentence makes the assumption that the leadership is already in decide and tell mode. This should be the moment when we stop and ask if decide and tell will achieve better business results than engaging the right people in decision forming.

Communication	Engagement
▪ Making connections	▪ Opening decision making and change to the right groups to:
▪ Sharing meaning	- add value
▪ Influencing mood / climate	- accelerate execution
▪ Setting context	- broaden ownership and sustainability
▪ Reinforcing status quo / hierarchy	▪ = power sharing
	▪ Disturbing status quo / suspending hierarchy

Figure 2.3   Communication and engagement

IS EMPLOYEE ENGAGEMENT A PROCESS OR AN INTEGRAL PART OF THE VALUES OF THE ORGANISATION?

At this point it is worth asking what kind of phenomenon employee engagement is.

Participants in my research said that first and foremost it is a management or leadership philosophy. CEOs I interviewed, and whose stories pepper the text, often commented that employee engagement, when it involved the considered involvement in decision making, required a shared philosophy about employee engagement among the leadership team and a conviction from the leader to take the perceived risk of opening a can of worms.

Employee engagement is also an outcome of making the philosophy a tangible day-to-day experience for people. And so if a CEO or supervisor is thinking how to open up decision making to get more value from people or to accelerate change, they may ask where they should start: an experimental employee engagement intervention is a good start. There are many examples in the text including the global freight carrier in Chapter 1, the European leisure company in Chapter 8 and the finance function of another global company in Chapter 10.

In these stories experiments in employee engagement were tried to overcome the stranglehold of the existing values. They were practical first steps in reform.

Employee engagement is also an addition to the way programmatic change is managed. Left to their own instincts most change programmes become temporary dictatorships. The principles of employee engagement can be introduced to the change process to enable the employees to add their contribution and drive speed of execution. Therefore it is also a process.

But first and foremost it must be an idea and a philosophy at the heart of the values and instincts of the organisation.

Employee engagement is also situational. There will be situations like the execution of a survival strategy where you need compliance, not necessarily with much understanding by those implicated. You just need the people to see that there is an emergency and there is not time to sit around in cosy dialogue. But as some of the stories told later illustrate, some leaders are experimenting with challenging this assumption of command-and-control leadership style and involving employees up front in solving the crisis in a much more inclusive way.

If you have decided that a purely instructional approach with little or no explanation is insufficient to get the people on board there are two ways to frame employee engagement (see Figure 2.4):

- Letting people onto the bridge or into the boardroom so that employees see things as the decision makers see them. This at least enables people to set decisions and implementation which affect them in the context of a broader idea. Much internal communication is based on this approach; explaining the strategy or decision made by a few to the many.

- Making considered judgements about which groups will add value if they are invited to contribute before decisions, change projects and strategy are finalised. This approach means that the planning of employee engagement needs to be done as an integral part of decision making rather than as part of post-decision-making implementation.

1 **The alignment model**: giving employees the same view/data/experience as decision makers

2 **The real engagement model**: opening up decision making to those who will add value and sustainability.

Figure 2.4   Two views of employee engagement

PARADOX OF BRAND

This chapter would be incomplete without the mention of brand and the paradox that the concept of brand may represent to employee engagement. Employee engagement involves considering who will add value if involved in the decision-making process. It involves inviting people to participate and influence routine decisions, bigger change and strategy. It may mean inviting people to 'personalise' the service they offer to customers and clients.

This is where the paradox of brand potentially emerges. There are some brand experiences, let's say in fast food, commoditised retail and maybe some low-end, no-frills travel, where you may want a virtually identical customer experience.

In others there will be more room for variation and personal interpretation at the point of customer interaction. Examples will include know-how and advisory firms like investment banks, upper-end retail banking, high fashion retail, airlines and travel companies choosing to differentiate through service and high-end hotels where some individuality and interpretation of the brand needs to be expressed above and beyond the prescribed brand experience. The task is to define the space for individuality and expression.

Two levels of decision about employee engagement need to be made when considering the brand experience:

• On forming or refreshing the brand proposition, to what degree is the exercise a top-down one as opposed to one where the wisdom and experience of the people is sought before the brand proposition is finalised. The leisure company story in Chapter 8 illustrates one approach to this question.

• In delivering the agreed brand proposition or experience what boundaries are there for different groups or categories of staff at different parts of the customer or client journey?

For the first question it seems to me that that this is a perfect opportunity to engage employees widely rather than relying on the opinions of a few experts and some tired senior executives who are probably out of touch with the place where the rubber hits the road.

The paradox lies in some of the assumed thinking among marketing people that they and their chums in the advertising and design agency are the experts who must make most of the decisions and then roll out the brand with some illusory programme dressed up as employee engagement. These are usually nothing more than information exercises put over with some opportunity to feed back. Feeding back after the proposition is set is not engagement at all: it is an opportunity for management to see what messages have been received and ram home reminders. CEOs and brand sponsors must be watchful for the authoritarian instincts of marketing-led approaches. They have a place in setting context but must not be allowed to dictate what employee engagement means in the organisation.

TEMPTATIONS OF THE SIRENS OF CULTURE MANAGEMENT

I have tried to emphasise that employee engagement is primarily an outcome of leadership, managerial and supervisory practices and in the previous section warned of the coercive instincts of marketing. It would be careless of me to omit a challenge to the siren of culture management which claims to be able to define desired behaviours and train and develop people into 'living desired behaviours'.

When I think for a minute about this proposition two things occur to me:

- It's a pretty coercive concept which sounds more at home in the collectivist states of old communism.

- The experience of most organisations in practising collectivist behaviour without the consent of the people is pretty dismal. Zillions are spent on 'people development and training' and much is successfully ignored.

The spirit of employee engagement is not about coercion and manipulation. Nor is it about a chaotic free-for-all. It is about inviting the right people to contribute to decision making to bring their wisdom and experience to bear and by so doing create a creative and compelling place to work.

CONDITIONS FOR SUCCESS

Finally in this chapter on definitions I summarise what employee engagement means for a company and four conditions for engagement to be successful.

Employee engagement drives value by inviting the people who deliver the end result to contribute to:

- everyday decision making;

- vision, strategy and implementation;

- crises, change and transformation;

- brand and service.

The conditions for success are:

- The sponsors of change or strategy have overtly and rationally considered and decided, as part of the design of the change, who will add value to the project.

- The sponsors of change or strategy have designed and governed the process and experience of engagement so that it sets the right invitation to leaders and employees to participate in and contribute to the change, whilst developing themselves in the context of the change.

- Even when the discretion open to participants to contribute is small, the engagement experience should be characterised by learning through self-discovery, rather than by instructional communication and indoctrination.

- There must be value and benefit for both the organisation and its members.

3 Four Approaches to Engaging Your People

From listening to bosses and employees I have concluded that there are four approaches to engage people in decision making: telling, selling, inclusion and co-creation. They are presented in Figure 3.1 with the likely outcome among leaders and employees.

Each approach has benefits, costs and risks and these should be weighed as part of the change or decision-making process. It seems from the stories of change which have been most successful that an effective leader has an intuitive model of approaches to engagement like the one shown in the figure and switches mode according to the ripeness of the moment. Less insightful leaders seem less able to switch mode because it bears so much on their personality. We explore the link between the climate of engagement in organisations and the personality of the leader in the next chapter.

WHEN MIGHT EACH APPROACH BE SUITABLE?

Telling the many what has been decided by the few

This may be the rational and effective choice for a leader who:

- is in a crisis situation with little time;

- already has a clear solution and knows that those implicated will support and execute an instructional approach, perhaps because it is long overdue. The people will support decisive action.

However, it should be noted that some leaders might hide behind or automatically adopt such an approach simply because it suits their preference.

Another situation where this approach may be suitable is where the existing culture has led people to expect and be comfortable with a tell approach. In this case, whilst other more inclusive approaches to engagement might add

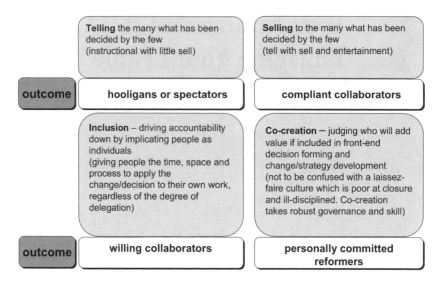

Source: *John Smythe and McKinsey & Company*

Figure 3.1   Four approaches to engaging people

more value, the transition to a more inclusive approach may be unaffordable or be seen as such. Many leaders see the tell approach as the safest and quickest route to effecting change. Leaders who grew up in a culture of command-and-control end up practising a tell mode of engagement because they have experienced little else for themselves. And that means most leaders. The tell mode is also predominant because of the obvious tension between time and inclusion of people in the decision-making process. The working assumption is that inclusion takes time, and is messy; 'a can of worms, which once opened is hard to close', as one interviewee for this book put it.

The culture of elitism compounds this assumption. Come the crisis and the leader is tempted to summon a crack internal team and/or a group of external consultants. And in many cases they will pit these two groups wittingly or unwittingly against each other, usually to demonstrate that the internal group is too implicated to be neutral. Crack teams guard their solutions jealously and are usually antipathetic to broader inclusion. Thus so much change is, and is perceived to be, imposed.

There is of course evidence that 'driving change through' can result in the changed behaviour required. However, others report that the instructional-tell approach dumbs down a workforce and makes them fearful of speaking out and experimenting.

By way of example, one of the organisations we interviewed, a major aerospace manufacturer, experienced a major quality breakdown on a subassembly plant which resulted in large components being delivered with faults which had to be rebuilt at the final assembly line. Fast action was required and a tell mode was adopted with specialists being dropped in to the offending parts of the line. In short order the quality problem had apparently been remedied and the cost of re-engineering fallen. But within months some of the best assembly engineers were walking to other local employers, most with years of service to this famous engineering brand. Morale, to use the old fashioned term, had slumped.

Interviews of the departing engineers revealed that the tell approach adopted during the period of crisis had been retained by managers and a formerly more inclusive approach to decision making had been replaced by an instructional style permitting little initiative or creativity to be expressed.

The employees felt that whilst the tell approach had been necessary to address the crisis, they also felt that the emergency measures should have been repealed to enable the climate of inclusion to return. Managers noticed that the quality checks which were normally part of the role of front-line staffs' role were not being carried out and quality was once again suffering. Employees reported that a climate of fear discouraged them from speaking out.

As quality again began to fall away the company took measures to re-establish the culture of inclusion which required managers and supervisors to relearn a more inclusive approach and workers to venture their professional opinions once again.

The leader of the intervention offered the view that faced with a dramatic crisis the temptation to get into an instructional fix-it mode was great, but that, with the benefit of hindsight, he would signal the end of the crisis and make explicit steps to welcome back the voices of the front line sooner. He also said that he would experiment with two, side-by-side approaches, one a traditional tell, the other based on co-creation.

The story of the magician revealing the parrot in the cage bit by bit by lifting its curtain

In my research on prevailing practices of engagement the tell mode was prominent in all 59 organisations and defended, particularly by older managers brought up on it.

One tale characterises many. A global, European-based insurer had an imaginative business strategy in an otherwise undifferentiated sector. The strategy contained a mix of initiatives involving changes to structure, job role, product and inevitably off-shoring and job cuts. Even managers close to the executive group were kept shrouded from seeing the big picture and employees reported experiencing individual changes without the benefit of explanation of how one change or initiative was connected to another. Nor had they any sense of what it all added up to.

Employee satisfaction scores were at an all-time low and customer service ratings were similarly poor. Mystified as to why a good story, albeit one with some pain, was not being told I asked the CEO.

The answer will be familiar to you. He was concerned that the investors would hold him to any story of change and had therefore decided that the safest policy was to hold the vision within an inner elite and let it emerge once the initiatives had had a positive effect. He was of the view that the inevitable negative slump in morale and customer satisfaction would be sustainable collateral damage. One executive described it as being like the magician slowly revealing the colours of the parrot bit by bit as he slowly lifted the curtain from its cage!

This CEO was firmly of the view that no value could be added by engaging employees in developing the strategy and that any benefit from spelling out the big picture – to put elements of the strategy in context – would be offset by possible negative judgements from the City if timescales and benefits were not delivered.

Many argued this line though this was perhaps an extreme example of the 'keep them in the dark and let them eat s**t' school of management.

Selling to the many what has been decided by the few

Selling to the many what has been decided by the few may be a rational choice in conditions similar to those where a tell mode is suitable but where the employee group is likely to be resistant to instruction and needs persuading to motivate and energise them. This may be because they have seen countless other tell attempts founder and need persuasion that this one has legs. A sell mode may also be a suitable precursor to a process of inclusion, particularly when a leader wants to sell the context for changes among a broad population where the operational impact is confined to relatively few.

However sell mode also seems to be the preferred choice of approach to employee engagement of many leaders brought up in the command-and-control style of leadership.

Too often the sell mode stands for little more than 'broadcasting' where a campaign approach is used in an attempt to mobilise people. Employees interviewed for my research reported that being cast as spectators rarely successfully implicates them unless the approach to engagement progresses to a process of inclusion where accountability is driven down to them.

Sell mode is often adopted in the mistaken belief that launching a change or strategy will bring it to life operationally.

Employees report on the vogue for internal marketing campaigns which come and go with little follow-up and thus many change processes are perceived to die after launch: 'after the road shows it was back to normal'. This will be familiar to many employees who attend the ritual of strategy/vision roll-out events in which executives strut their stuff.

It is perhaps easy to dismiss executive grandstanding. But there is a balance to be struck between hero commander figures who seem to have all the answers and leaders who are invisible. It's all a question of timing. The leader needs to constantly judge which mode of engagement will add value at each stage of the change process.

Inclusion – driving accountability down

Driving accountability down means implicating people as individuals. It means allowing people the time and space to apply a company-wide change to their own work and their own development, even if they had little input to the nature of the change or decision.

This is essential when implementing the operational consequences of a change or strategy where deep understanding and insight is needed by those who must make it work. It is also key where local input is required to tailor or adapt a common approach. It may also allow for surprising discoveries and insights to emerge from groups who feel valued and safe in offering ideas.

To illustrate an inclusive approach let's take the bold example of the global data corporation which was famously hit simultaneously by the dot com bust, massive competition and a period of mismanagement characterised by over extension of the brand, proliferation of unprofitable product and a free-for-all management style.

A share price collapse resulted and the business was not far off disaster. A new administration moved quickly on cost reduction, staff cuts and drastic streamlining of the product portfolio. Off-shoring product development was also a no-brainer when a technology task in the UK might cost £85 000 versus £14 000 in India.

Product development processes were standardised and sales and service operations merged. None of this is surprising. Faced with the same, many a leader would have decided what to do and told everyone what was happening. Indeed in this case the business case was presented to the company under the banner of the 'last chance saloon'.

What is surprising and interesting about this story is that in parallel to the 'hard cop' activity was a programme of inclusion open to every employee around this global company. Called Fast Track this process was designed to engage everyone in identifying the issues or blockers which might disable the transformation.

The transformation comprised a number of themes including product streamlining, customer service, internal customer relations and shared services. Over 5000 issues or blockers identified by staff were clustered into a few actionable work streams and the work of addressing them given back to well-governed employee teams.

Being a technology company the engagement process included a global meeting of employees in which every location was connected by satellite TV. The process of engagement was described by some staff as a 'catharsis, a visible passing of the wreckage of the old company and the genesis of the new'.

During the transformation, employees were able to log onto a specially designated change web channel and track the impact of their own ideas upon the transformation. A clever idea as many an engagement initiative is tarnished because employees cannot see if and how their ideas have influenced the change process.

Alongside Fast Track this company ran an HR support process, called the Transformational Way, which provided explicit guidance and development for employees on skills and behaviour required to survive in the new world.

The company made a rapid recovery and claims that its twin track, hard cop, soft cop approach was critical. Employees I interviewed emphasised the importance of making clear that this twin track was part of one strategy. They reported that many colleagues saw them as two disconnected initiatives and among these cynicism was higher.

There is much natural inclusion in the workplace whether practiced intuitively by leaders and supervisors or introduced via work improvement practices such as quality programmes, six sigma, lean engineering and self-directed work teams, where as the name implies the team is made responsible for its own work.

Indeed this whole concept of broader inclusion is hardly new. It has surfaced under various labels across the last 50 years. What is new is the shift in expectations which people have of work. No longer do they have job security to bind in their loyalty, nor do they have the promise of index-linked pensions (except of course in the public sector). Loyalty has no trade off and employees are exercising a right to roam from employer to employer. Smart employers are recognising that the day-to-day experience of being a meaningful part of decision making helps to create an attractive place to work.

Including people in managing their own work has always been highest in engineering and manufacturing, service and operational settings where the people have more natural discretion both to improve or, if they choose, to sabotage. The car industry led the way in involving people in their day-to-day work with Volvo being one of the first to replace an assembly line with units of production.

Aerospace has been another pioneer. When, post 9/11, the world's aerospace industry was catapulted into almost instant recession, a huge engineering company and industry leader faced an evaporation of orders. Orders which take years to win. The company faced a major crisis. But amidst the search for cost cutting lay the glimmer of an opportunity to tackle the industrial relations problems which had beset the company since the rise of the aero industry after World War 2. Each manufacturing site had to justify its claim to exist as cuts could not be avoided and only those which could demonstrate a more flexible approach would survive.

This rigidity, reminiscent of the car industry of the 1970s in the UK, had to be dealt with. And perhaps in large part due to 9/11, there was a window of opportunity. A new boss from GE and a workforce, who saw that something had to give, made change possible.

Existing working practices prevented workers from one skill from helping out on another task and frequently a hiccup, which virtually any one skilled worker could fix, resulted in lengthy delays while the designated specialist was located. In addition the traditional role of foreman meant that critical information about prioritisation and stock levels remained locked up in men who had a vested interest in holding on to that information.

In response the role of foreman was abolished, a new SAP information system introduced and a team-based system of working introduced which vested most production decisions to the teams.

These decisions included:

- prioritising the manufacturing sequence according to customer needs;
- ordering all stock on an on-time basis;
- the abolition of hated clocking in, replaced by time sheets;
- rostering their own work including holidays;
- quality.

The workers in one site helped to design much of the team system including the design of a 'work in progress' monitor allowing them to monitor their own progress and pass the baton on quickly to the next shift in shift handover meetings.

The improvements stopped bottlenecks, hastened delivery and quality, reduced cost of manufacture (via reduction in consumables cost) and created a more adaptable workforce who wanted to extend their multiple skills across all demarcation lines. The workers reported that the diversity of work and greater responsibility coupled with greater access to data and the ability to influence their work made the job much more interesting.

However some of the workers I interviewed had reservations. In darker moments they wondered if the price of greater inclusion in decision making affecting their normal jobs may be the thin end of the wedge of a process designed to get them to accept other efficient practices which would cost benefits or jobs. As one worker succinctly put it: 'I feel I have greater control over my day job but less control over my life.'

Co-creation

The fourth and last approach to engagement is co-creation. Co-creation means identifying and working with those who will add value if they are included in decision forming and change and strategy development before decisions are made or plans for change are finalised.

Many people I interviewed talked about co-creation as their aspired mode of engagement and in my McKinsey and Company research into engagement there were many stories illustrating attempts by CEOs to practise co-creation.

Co-creation is a good choice of approach to engagement when:

- The sponsor(s) of change of strategy or a unit head knows things must move on and has an idea of how things must be better but cannot, through analysis alone, determine the solution and must ask others who possess the wisdom and experience to contribute.

- The sponsor(s) of change or decision makers have a perfectly good solution but sense that the population to be affected may look at the problem or opportunities from a different angle and produce better solutions, or at least solutions which become owned by those who will be affected by the change and must implement it.

Two stories from my research illustrate co-creation. The first is the story of CEO Jack who starts off a journey of change in a traditional manner but has a 'road to Damascus moment' and switches to a different and more inclusive path.

Let me set the scene. A CEO is determined to 'mobilise his people' behind a breakthrough strategy on which his reputation rests. The cameo features an initial one-way monologue from the CEO Jack to his communication director, and Jack's later reflections and the musings of a supervisor called Johnny. Names have been changed!

Scene 1: Jack briefs his communication director

The change team has completed the strategy/plan/repositioning. I want it campaigned to everyone.

Let's kick it off with a major business conference to raise its profile. We'll need the whole exec team up on stage to show that we're all united behind it.

We'll need a theme: How about 'Changing to Win'?

Then I want road shows across Europe and cascades in every place of work.

You know the maxim – tell them what you're going to tell them, tell them and then tell them what we've told them.

I want to capture hearts and minds and mobilise everyone behind this strategy.

We need metrics: I want to know that our messages have been received and acted upon. And I want the performance management process to align people's goals with the strategy.

Oh and our people need to be brand ambassadors for the new positioning for the firm. We all need to be singing off the same song sheet and walk the talk!

All of this should precede a multi-million-pound marketing spend across direct marketing, PR, government relations and advertising.

We're going to transform this business by Christmas!

Scene 2: Hi, my name is Johnny. I'm a senior supervisor

I'm a Change to Win pathfinder. Is this the focus group on 'Changing to Win'? I've just come back from the big conference and the road shows. They were terrific and I did some great networking. I had a great time.

But I can't remember much apart from the hangover ... it was wall-to-wall presentations about ... err ... well a new strategy, new customer metrics, restructuring again. Isn't it funny most new strategies end up as restructures.

But it's OK as I've got this 70-deck slide show to cascade to my reports, which I knew I was going to get so we know we don't have to pay too much attention. Most of us spend time thinking how disjointed the top team are. They can't bear not being the centre of attention so when one is speaking the rest gaze around displaying body language straight from a bad marriage.

I've got to take all my teams through this stuff so we get high marks on the comprehension test ... our code for Jack's feedback to Jack!

Now it's back to the routine. This stuff will be last year's fad soon enough.

But there'll be no getting away from the torrent of electronic garbage ... sorry internal communication about it from Jack on the new Change to Win intranet site.

You should see the ad campaign promising levels of customer service which we know just can't be sustained. At least we saw it in advance so we're braced for the complaints.

Where's lunch then?

Scene 3: Jack reflects after a night in the bar at one of the conference venues

I caught a cold with Change to Win. My executive team had never really agreed about it and when I went around the regions most saw it as another ill-fated initiative, especially the customers who wondered whose idea the ad campaign was!

I managed to pin one of our supervisors down in the conference centre bar in Krakow. He gave me the usual snow job for a while then admitted that he thought I hadn't a chance of implementing it because it was the usual show and tell which everyone pretends to enjoy but feels no connection with it. He said it's like being a spectator at someone else's party. I said but this is your company, your pension plan. But he looked at me as if I was from another planet. It was then that I realised that to him I may as well be from another planet.

It was just what I needed. For once someone had had the courage to tell it like it is.

I realized that it is not just the shareholders who I have to engage with. It's our people too or my strategies will end up as so much waste paper. Plus I know I have to reinvent what we mean by engaging people in our change processes.

Our old style of engaging people meant telling, selling and marketing at our people. It was very parent–child. I realised all it was doing was neutralising people and sucking the energy out of them.

What we need is a communication culture where people want to implicate themselves voluntarily in the change. We realised that the old experience of tell/sell/egotainment became the customer experience. And conversely if we could engage our people more creatively and respectfully that experience would become the customer experience.

Scene 4: Johnny participating in a real-time web-based focus group on the Change to Win site.

I was so incensed with those smoothies in marketing telling the CEO what a triumph it all was. I had to tell him that the whole pantomime of road shows and so on goes straight above people's heads – that they are more for the benefit of his ego than anything else. I thought that's it, I've had it. But he listened to every word and we had a few drinks

> *together. It was the best communication I've ever had here. He said it was the best he'd ever had.*
>
> *Anyway the next thing is I'm asked (along with 20 other supervisors) to re-do the customer research ourselves. We got given a budget and an advisor who helped us decide how to go about it. We decided to do a fly-on-the-wall documentary and we filmed our guys at work in customers' premises and got the most amazing impromptu opinions from customers. I always used to think that research firms made up all that stuff and never believed a word of it. Management used to use it as a weapon. But the real thing from the horse's mouth made me cringe.*
>
> *Then we put together these workshops for all our colleagues called 'The Bad Service Journey' and pretty soon everyone twigged that we are the bad service journey. They believed it because it was us presenting not management.*
>
> *It didn't stop there though. In the second phase we had to develop possible 'solution paths' to remedy the bad service journey. We had to imagine that we held the change budget and prioritise solutions according to the impact on customer retention. Then we had to design an implementation toolbox so that we could take this back to our own work areas.*
>
> *Finally we had to take our best solution to the change board. All the workshop leaders were there. Each of us had to explain and champion our solution and we all voted on each others work.*
>
> *The change board had adopted some of the practices from Work Out – You Know, that GE process where proposals are put to a board and they have to say yes, no or give a little more time for scoping.*
>
> *From there the change board honed the solutions and it is all being implemented through us. You can imagine how differently we all felt this time. This was our work shining through.*

Whether or not you have a road-to-Damascus experience like Jack you may be asking what are the constituent parts of designing an engagement intervention which will add value and be worth the time and effort involved.

The second story illustrating the choice of co-creation features a utility which had to transform an engineering culture into a customer-friendly culture. But first it had to chop 40 per cent of its costs – a difficult task in any business but doubly so in a public utility in which unions were traditionally very strong. The CEO knew that the traditional approach to cost cutting as a top-down senior management exercise would have the appearance of speed and decisiveness.

But this CEO was a male in his fifties and he had experienced the long aftermath of top-down command-driven cost cutting. He had experienced the rancour in employees and in communities and he wanted to try a different approach.

That approach was co-creational. His aim was not a free-for-all democracy, but a reasoned and well-governed process of inclusion of some of the right people in the business in dealing with the costs crisis. In the early days unions were sceptical to say the least.

Sceptical because even if they could be sure that the management meant what it said, co-creation looked like it would cut across their relationship with employees. Their power base was at stake. Management had to convince them that they meant what they said and that they would be a part of the process.

To do this they turned to the services of a well-known UK college, Ruskin, to prepare management and unions alike to participate in the process. Being renowned as left of centre in political terms, Ruskin inspired confidence in the unions which took the risk of participating.

Meanwhile the company established business unit councils across all its activities to govern the process of involvement locally. An overarching 20-strong council stands above the business units populated by representatives from the units. Every aspect of the change was put through these councils. The only non-negotiable was that 40 per cent of costs had to come off. Where and how were questions put to the employee councils.

Management naturally had a view about how it would achieve the cuts but the CEO and his colleagues parked their solution whilst staff, equipped with skills and concepts familiar to management such as net present value, profit and loss and the like worked on theirs.

The CEO reported that there was no 'bottom drawer of data' which was held back from staff. He operated an open-door policy, making staff welcome if they wanted to go through files and data relevant to a challenge set to councils – an invitation regularly taken up.

Challenges tackled included apparently intractable issues like the consolidation of three laboratories and three call centres into one, the merger and consolidation of numerous field engineering centres and the standardisation of terms and conditions which would result in some workers losing pay and conditions.

Any one of these and others could have triggered industrial action. Indeed if tackled in the traditional way almost certainly would have. But in a ballot on all the issues, staff voted in favour of the changes, albeit narrowly. But the positive vote was considered extraordinary given the sensitivity of the issues being tackled.

The management team were pleasantly surprised by many of the solutions proposed by the councils. Looked at from the perspectives of staff, the company's interests and the impact on the community of the various options open, the councils repeatedly saw solutions which management had not thought of. 'We look down on the problem. Staff look at it from a totally different perspective and, not surprisingly, see solutions invisible to us.'

Of course the councils do not have carte blanche to take decisions. They have to weigh the data, propose multiple solutions and then argue their chosen path, sometimes prevailing, sometimes not.

In any event the executive team is in no doubt that a co-creational approach has enabled the organisation to make necessary and painful changes (including 2000 lost jobs) with no strikes, no service interruptions, no lost legal cases and with plenty of new ideas implemented.

This company is now in the post-crisis phase of building and the CEO wants to extend the idea of inclusion to every level of leadership so that it becomes one of the 'capabilities and duties of citizenship, both for leaders and all staff'. This he reckons will be a big challenge. 'We have to leave behind the foreman model of supervision, which is based on an authoritarian model of leadership, which is very ingrained, and replace it with an inclusive model. I expect it to take a generation, but we are making a start.'

CO-CREATION – AN ACCEPTABLE RISK?

I have illustrated the co-creational approach with two examples featuring leaders who exhibited great courage to go against the grain. In both cases many other more conventionally minded leaders would probably have selected a tell or sell approach. Indeed many senior people I interviewed stoutly defended doing so. And some refused to countenance that a co-creational approach to change was an acceptable risk. Yet these stories, among many others I encountered are a living example of the benefits to be gained from co-creation.

In fact those who take the risk are in no doubt that it was a risk worth taking, pointing to the valuable insights brought by employees and the increased sustainability of changes co-created by some of those implicated. One client, Patrick O'Sullivan (CFO of Zurich Financial Services at time of writing), with whom we have worked regularly, reckons that he will involve a minimum of 25 per cent of employees in turning around damaged businesses arguing that he simply doesn't know where many of the bodies are buried and that even if he did, involving quite significant numbers helps to create a 'tipping point' (to quote author Malcolm Gladwell) in the levels of popular acceptance of change.

I am not arguing that the co-creational approach is the one-size-fits-all option. Indeed the insights I would like people to draw from this chapter are firstly that making an explicit choice of approach to engagement is better than an irrational automatic adoption of an approach which may not be fit for purpose. The next chapter looks at this in a little more detail. The second insight is that the smart leader seems to use a mixture of approaches at different times and situations and with different audiences.

Finally, Figure 3.2 provides direct quotes from senior interviewees illustrating the four approaches to engagement and Figure 3.3 gives guidance on the right approach to engagement in the form of a checklist.

a) Telling people what has been decided (instructional with little sell)	b) Selling to the many what has been decided by the few (tell with a sell and some entertainment)
'Even though our CEO has vision, it is never fully revealed … we have to drip feed operational decisions when it suits … like the magician slowly revealing the parrot in the cage.' *HR Director* 'Engagement is basically no more than a method of gaining compliance.' *BU Head*	'Means identifying and planning who needs to be part of accepting a decision/strategy.' *HR Director* 'The wise ruler listens to express decisions in the frame of reference of the people.' *CEO* 'Energetic followship depends on trust: the credibility of the leaders.' *CEO* 'Enabling other people to discover what you have already discovered/decided by giving them a taste of the experience and insights which the sponsor team has had.' *Adviser*
c) Inclusion: driving accountability down by implicating people as individuals (giving people the time, space and process to apply the change/decision to their own work, regardless of the degree of delegation)	d) Co-creation: working with those who will add value if included in decision forming and change/strategy development (not to be confused with a laissez-faire culture which is poor at closure and ill-disciplined. Co-creation takes robust governance and skill

'Engagement means driving ownership down to individuals by asking people to implicate themselves in their own personal professional journeys in the context of the organisational journey.' *CEO*
 	
'Giving people the space to make sense of the change such that they can identify how much they need to stretch to contribute.' *Change Director*
 	
'You have to judge the trade-off between apparent immediacy of execution and personal commitment which comes from inviting people through exploration, engagement and enaction.' *Adviser*
 	
'We repeat the self-diagnosis in each country even though we know what needs to be done because it creates local energy.' *Adviser*
	'Democratising strategy, change and operational work so that those who must sustain it are implicated in decision forming.' *CEO*
	
	'That means considering who to enfranchise in:
	  - creating or sharing the burning platform/ opportunity for change;
	  - content design (who holds the key to the safe);
	  - adapting implementation locally.' *CEO*
	
	'The greater the lack of clarity about need for change/direction the more you need to take risks in engaging the right people.' *CEO*
	
	'You need to distinguish between catch-up improvement strategies and sector leadership where you must make a leap of faith and decide who you will take with you on the leap.' *Adviser*
	
	'The CEO becomes more Guide than God.' *CEO*
	
	'The trouble at the top is that our egos make it hard for us to make the personal transformations which we are asking the organisation to make.' *Group HR Director*

Source: John Smythe and McKinsey & Company

Figure 3.2   Four choices of approach to engaging people in change and strategy

Checklist.

Q   What is the situation: is this crisis, recovery, growth, acquisition or opportunity for transformation?

Q   Who else will be a part of the inner tent and be seen as a role model of the change?

Q   What is my/our interpretation of engagement. Do we share a view?

Q   What is my/our track record in engaging leadership and everyone in recent strategy/change?

Q   Looking at the change/strategy now being considered what are the likely horizons of activity? For each horizon which specific groups would, if engaged, add value:
*   to substance/content;
*   to implementation;
*   by acting as vanguards for the process.

Q   What principles do we want to set for the design of the engagement process, for example:
*   Is it radical enough; are participants reporting being disposed to action?
*   Does it provide participants sufficient space to reflect on their own personal growth in the context of the change?
*   Is the engagement sufficiently relevant to people's day job to produce actionable ideas?
*   Can participants see their contributions influencing the process?
*   Is the formal communication process providing context and coherence for the change/strategy as a whole?

Q   Do I/we role model the espoused engagement style(s) in our everyday interactions with each other and our colleagues? How aware am I/we of these everyday styles?

Q   In constructing shared scripts about the change/strategy have we articulated our approach to engaging people alongside clarity about:
*   rationale/market drivers for the change;
*   outcomes required;
*   route chosen;
*   rationale for the chosen approach for engagement;
*   timescales for the change/strategy.

Source: John Smythe and McKinsey & Company

Figure 3.3   Making the right choice of approach to engaging leaders and employees in the development of strategy and change

4 The Irrationality of Leaders in Engaging Their People in Strategy and Change

The practice of engaging people in change and strategy seems to be an aspect of leadership which is driven more by impulse rather than by reason. Most interviewees in my research into employee engagement struggled at the outset of the interview to articulate clearly what they felt their own or their organisation's approach to engagement to be.

There was a wide range of immediate responses, from 'achieving alignment and understanding and making people feel involved' to interpretations suggesting a more inclusive approach such, as 'involving people in co-creating the change'.

Their concepts about engagement became clearer to me as the interviewer, and to the interviewees themselves, as their stories about the organisation unfolded. In many instances interviewees simply had not been asked that question before. Many were unsure about the difference between communication and engagement.

Interviewees who held functional roles (HR, communication, organisational development, change) spoke about engagement as if they were observers or agents of a process directed or shaped elsewhere, usually by the executive team. The sponsors of change themselves (the CEO, COO or BU head) spoke of engaging others in more personal terms but surprised themselves as they made their own approach to engagement explicit to themselves and to me in the telling of their stories about change.

CHOICE OF APPROACH TO EMPLOYEE ENGAGEMENT IS OFTEN IMPULSIVE

For most leaders engagement is one of those impulsive, taken-for-granted concepts, which reflects and is indivisible from their leadership persona because it is habitual. For many leaders their impulsive approach to engaging employees has either generally served them well enough not to give pause for thought, or has at some level been problematic.

This is not to say that impulsive choices of approaches to engagement always result in a poor outcome for the organisation – far from it – they may be good enough most of the time. But it is to say that overt consideration of the most appropriate approach to engagement may well add value or at least make the choice of approach to engagement clear to a wider team around the leader.

Take for example James, a new BU head. Six months or so into a new job as BU head James finds himself reflecting in our interview that the style of engagement which he had employed was an instinctive choice. His instinctive style of engagement was co-creational among top- and mid-level leaders and distinctly 'tell with some sell' for everyone else, certainly in the early stages of 'strategic feasibility'.

In the organisation concerned, given the level of change necessary, it was a perfectly rational approach for the first phase of the restructuring required. It was also a conservative paternal style which was familiar to the population. But, in the interview, James recognised that he was about to make a transition from implementing technical and structural change to one where he aspired to create a customer-centric culture. It occurred to him that his default engagement style (fairly traditional top-down) might not be fit for purpose after all and that other styles of engagement, which he had not yet even considered, might help him accelerate the behavioural changes needed.

Another interviewee, a change director of a part of a European aerospace firm where quality was paramount to customer safety, expressed no doubts about the wisdom of a highly directive change accompanied by an instructional approach to engaging people.

But, by the end of his story, he had decided that whilst the instructional nature of the change had resulted in compliant collaboration, it may also have created 'robots' who, in effect, would only respond to instruction.

In the telling of his story, at the point when the immediate crisis had passed, he observed that a more participative and creative workforce would be needed to 'accelerate the transformation to achieve the next level of performance'. He also recalled that highly skilled workers had started to leave in protest at the newly instructional regime.

He further reflected that his change team could have consciously considered more of a twin track to engaging the people in the process. By way of remedial action he then described engaging specialists in cultural change to re-engage people emotionally to 'regain their trust impaired during the brutality of the early part of the change'.

In both of these stories the individuals made reference to the heat of the moment and the sense of rightness about their instinctive choice of style of engagement. In the latter case, the change director also commented on the strong influence that strategy consultants had had on the approach to engagement, commenting that the consultants' values and instincts favoured speed, secrecy, elitism and a directive-tell approach.

Beware the values of consultants

He and others reflected on the benefit and dangers of the values of consultants who brought their own organisational values with them on client assignments. Some described this positively, citing that the can-do, solution-oriented values of some consultants rubbed off on the inmates of the host company. Others described their influence as more akin to the infections which arrive with adventurers and explorers to afflict native populations. Either way it is worth the time of those procuring the services of consultants to assess the whether they want a values clash to 'shake things up' or a fit to ease the path.

Switching to co-creational approach to employee engagement

Another CEO of a global science-based engineering company became emboldened in his choice of engagement style during the course of a transformation. He described how in the early days of the reform he engaged the top 50 in a difficult decision by giving them the same data which he and his immediate team had used to decide how to consolidate the group. This wider group came to similar conclusions as the CEO.

He had invited the broader leadership group to 'be the board' and using the same data as the board to consider what options existed in the best interests of the company. In his book *The Wisdom of Crowds* (2005, Abacus), James Surowiecki takes this concept to the level of the nation-state using the idea of 'deliberative polling': voters are presented with the same issues facing government and asked what policy options exist to address the issues. Back in the engineering company the next level of leadership played the game and recommended a dramatic restructuring which they knew would cost many of them their jobs. Had the solution been unilaterally imposed there would have been blood on the floor. Having been party to the decisions, executives who would have to leave were keen to oversee the handover confident that they had a much better story on their job history than if they had just been 'let go': they had let go of themselves.

Later the CEO described a 'daring judgement' to include a yet wider management team of 180 or so in co-creating group-wide strategy. The switch in engagement style was not explicitly explained or debated with close colleagues at the time and the ensuing co-creational activity was not fully understood or recognised as an important change of dynamic. This

57

highlighted that the invitation to participate has to be very explicit indeed, in the same way that a good chairperson lays out the ground rules of a meeting.

These stories typify the impulsive and very personal choices that are made by leaders about the style of engagement, based on their previous experience, role models and assumptions. Judgements made by leaders about whom and how to engage may not be wholly rational, considered or overtly part of the development of the change or strategy. They tend to be impulsive and tacit choices reflecting the instincts and experiences of the leader or leadership group.

So what; does the irrationality of leaders in their choice of approach to engagement make any difference to business performance?

Clearly in the case of the aerospace manufacturer referred to earlier the leader regretted adopting a tell approach and felt that although it initially arrested quality problems it was not sustainable and soon resulted in damage to the business.

Let's look at this question in a little more depth. Because the choice of approach to engagement is often impulsive and a product of personal preference and previous experience, the top team almost certainly do not share the same instincts about engagement. Different approaches to engagement will emerge as will different stories about the change and the team will both appear dysfunctional and be dysfunctional.

In a top team where negotiation and agreement is often tacit, perhaps because the team has worked together for a while and norms are in place, or because the leader is used to ramming things through, underlying disagreement may only emerge in scripts adopted by members of the team when they communicate and engage with others below them.

Thus differing styles of engagement in any team often only become apparent in informal and formal communication during implementation.

Team members form private versions or scripts of the stories going on in the team. And very often these scripts and stories about the meeting and decisions are only made explicit when the individual team members attempt to communicate their version of events when they have returned to their own part of the organisation.

As there has not been explicit agreement driven through the team by the leader about either the story or the approach to engagement, the impression given to employees by their returning bosses is a fragmented one where they are often seen, in retrospect, to be at sixes and sevens.

Unless the leader can drive things along by sheer force of personality his plan, however correct, will remain obscured by the many different stories which will flourish in the absence of a story negotiated as part of the decision-making process.

And this is all too often the case when leaders see communication as being an exercise in delivery or presentation once decisions or change plans have been supposedly completed by one person or a small group.

There is a misplaced assumption that communicators or marketeers will be able to make sense of a jumble of unfinished decisions and turn them into a convincing story. Sometimes a gifted story maker can do just that. But even when a communicator has this ability the sponsors of the change themselves are still left with a fragmented and incomplete story in their heads. And, as role models, will soon be in conflict with the 'official' version being communicated. Nor is it simply an incomplete story. It is an incomplete decision.

59

This failure to negotiate a decision and the subsequent shared story among the decision-making group indicates either that the leader wants to keep people in the dark or it means that the leader has not yet grasped that effective communication starts in their meetings with proper negotiation about decisions and a rational choice between approaches to engagement.

To make a rational choice between the four approaches to engagement (tell, sell, inclusion, co-creation; see Chapter 3) requires negotiation which does not conclude with the first flush of apparent agreement – the spirit of agreement – but with the negotiation of a single coherent story which the whole group constructs together; and in so doing determines what is agreed, what is confused and where genuine disagreement lies, allowing for further negotiation or closure by the leader.

Source: Getty Images

THE METAPHOR OF THE PEACE TREATY

I like to use the metaphor of the peace treaty. No skilled peace negotiator allows the parties to leave the room until every detail is hammered out so that there is contractual and emotional agreement and detailed discussion about how the groups being represented at the meeting will be engaged in the process.

Negotiations about change, strategy or vision and other company matters are no different. Yet too often both the story making and the engagement planning are assumed to be the work of others or not necessary.

Inclusion of story making and the planning of engagement as an integral and overt part of decision making and change formation means that bosses are having to think through who will add value if included up front and identify how implementation may be accelerated by robust planning of employee engagement and accompanying communication. To draw from politics, a democracy must not only work but be widely seen to work to generate the participation of the groups implicated.

Negotiations over decisions or changes frequently stop at the spirit-of-agreement stage. Those at the centre of the decision making may be tired or bored or tacitly aware that the so-called agreement will fall apart once it is print, unless so ambiguously worded that it allows everyone to interpret it as they fancy; which of course explains why many 'after the fact' internal communication exercises are Delphic exercises in obfuscation.

In answering the question 'Does the irrationality of leaders in their approach to engagement matter?', I contend that leaders who fully negotiate the decisions, however painful, agree the content of the story and plan the engagement of everyone who is implicated will have a much greater chance of a successful project.

This is another way of saying that leaders (at every level) must also pay attention to planning the execution of their plans as well as their origination. But I am adding that the origination and implementation of decisions and plans also requires planning the engagement of wider populations early on in the life of the decision or plan.

THE CHIEF ENGAGEMENT OFFICER: THE CEO

Thus I have coined the phrase the 'chief engagement officer'. Every leader, from chief executive officer to call centre supervisor now has the added function of chief engagement officer. The job description involves being responsible for ensuring the planning and execution of the engagement of their people in day-to-day performance and change.

It means understanding that day-to-day decisions and change are incomplete until the planning and execution of engagement is concluded as part of their decision-making process. I refer to this as completing the decision-making cycle and it is shown in Figure 4.1.

Think about the decision-making cycle as the journey of a decision or change process. At the beginning you have a problem or opportunity to

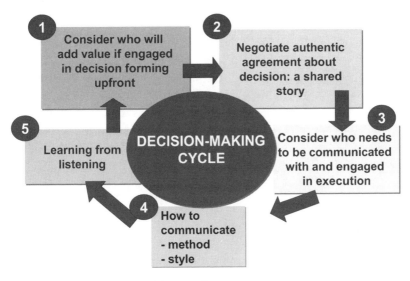

Figure 4.1   Decision-making cycle

address. At this point it might be worth reflecting on the typical journey which your decision making takes. Could you draw the journey? I wonder how explicitly conscious it is. And I wonder how the pattern of your decision-making journeys evolved. Most likely it is a reflection of the role models you have experienced and the outcome of all your experimentation. In other words you, like the rest of us, have a typical decision journey or cycle which is pretty automatic to you; but much analysed by those on the receiving end – your fellow leaders and employees. The Kremlin watchers will be watching and predicting your decision making based on your past form.

Source: Istockphoto/Justin Horrocks

Leaders often naively think that their deliberations are more hidden than they really are. Most employee groups are good at sensing what's going on behind closed doors and official announcements rarely come as much of a surprise. Like the stock market, the general population has usually priced the news into the stock price before the official announcement.

The decision-making cycle diagram is the centrepiece of Chapter 5. It is an attempt to express diagrammatically how the planning and execution of the engagement of the right people in day-to-day performance and change can be an integral part of the decision-making process.

5 Why Employee Engagement Matters – The Missing Half of Decision Making

DECISION MAKERS MUST CONSIDER HOW TO ENGAGE

In the last chapter I dwelt on how much leadership behaviour is impulsive or habitual and therefore can be irrational. In this chapter I argue for the inclusion of planning the engagement of those implicated in a decision or change in the initial decision-forming process, before the die is cast.

Let's step back. Everyone communicates at home and at work so what is so difficult about it?

All of us are left confused when another party walks away from a meeting or expresses apparent understanding, even agreement, and then behaves in an unpredictable fashion. In organisations leaders are frustrated that despite waves of formal 'tell and sell' communication, their people don't get the strategy. What can explain this phenomenon?

Part of the answer lies in my contention that no operational decisions or grand plan can be said to be complete until the decision makers or sponsors have thought through how to engage those who are implicated in the decision/change.

Most decision makers stop the process of decision making when the spirit of agreement is reached and it is assumed that the scripts in people's heads are the same. The members of the meeting rely on the scripts in their heads, their own notes or, worse still, electronic minutes being produced by someone else.

All too often a hapless communicator will attempt to make *post hoc* sense of what the decision makers have said; and the population of the organization will receive the official text from the formal communication source and hear the chaotic scripts playing from their line bosses who have returned from management meetings to brief them formally or on the run.

I believe that the missing half of decision making which falls under the heading of communication/engagement comprises three critical responsibilities for leaders:

- *The story completes the negotiation.* Negotiation of the detail of the decision beyond the spirit of the agreement so that participants in the decision-making process have exchanged their understanding of the decision such that differences and hidden disagreement become clear and further negotiation is seen to be necessary. This in turn enables a sustainable agreement to be reached and a 'shared story' to be created, which reflects the authenticity of the negotiation they have participated in.

- *Agreeing who to engage before the die is cast.* Agreeing as part of the decision-making process whether the decision/change being discussed will benefit from up-front involvement of colleagues drawn from outside the executive or change team. This means asking the question, who else will add value?

- *Upfront planning of communication improves decision making.* Whether a process of engagement is undertaken or not, planning communication early on will improve the quality and pace of decision making. For example, in a merger between two banks the requirement for all streams of integration to have an engagement and communication plan to obtain management approval, prevented the early cancellation of a catering contract which would have signalled the closure of an office before the workers affected had been communicated with in the right way, affecting morale and the credibility of the integration process.

  It is still rare for these three core components to form an intrinsic part of the decision-making process. Too often, work on planning the engagement of or communication with people is performed outside and usually after decisions and plans are formed and made.

  It is commonly viewed as a secondary activity and is often done by specialists such as communicators, marketeers and the like. Divorced from the decision-making process it is seen as being inferior work to real decision making.

My argument is that no policy, decision, change or plan is complete unless these three core components form an intrinsic part of the decision-forming process.

Leaders brought up in the command-and-control school of management still assume that communication is an after-the-fact activity. There is also a tendency to see the duty to communicate as being largely about presenting and performing.

BUILDING ENGAGEMENT AND COMMUNICATION PLANNING INTO DECISION MAKING: A PRACTICAL MODEL

So how do leaders turn the theory into practice?

Let's take the case of the European investment bank which was haemorrhaging key staff to competitors. Internal investigations and exit interviews led management to believe that part of the problem could be put down to the 'macho management style' of some department heads. In a world where only profit had any significance it was not too surprising that most successful department heads did the business first and saw management as an afterthought.

They had grown up in a world where command-and-control was the only leadership model, the only variation being just how macho you could make it. As it was the universal model nobody had complained too much and in any event it hardly mattered which bank you worked for, it was pretty much the same anywhere.

The result was much the same, you put up with it on the way up then you dished it out to those below you on their way up.

People in this bank started to leave, but not just for more money over the road. They were leaving because of the way they were being managed. More specifically they were leaving because of the unilateral manner in which many newly promoted department bosses took decisions on the fly, mirroring the transactional instincts of their day job as traders and deal makers.

Instincts and culture take a long time to shift. But in this case we took a behavioural approach to the issue. We avoided the temptation of the 'training them better' route. We had learnt from a previous investment bank encounter that traders and training, like oil and water, do not mix. These are people with limited attention spans.

But each had some specific managerial issues to resolve. And none wanted to come top of the bad boss league any more. And with more and more league tables of 'great places to work', like those published by *The Times* in the UK and *Fortune* magazine, managing people well started to have some cachet.

We asked team leaders to draw the process by which they would normally reach and execute a decision on the managerial issue facing them. This was novel for them because it gave them personal insight into the flow of their own decision-making journey. Later many framed their drawings to remind themselves how they scoped out an issue or opportunity, how they decided who they would ask to contribute to its resolution, how they tested solutions and how they went about trying to execute it and communicate about it.

By so doing most had drawn some insight about the likely impact of their decision making and communication styles on their colleagues and reports; they were eager to improve both the process of decision making and communication planning, and their styles of communication.

Using the decision-making cycle diagram (shown again in Figure 5.1) we then asked each to build an alternative route to making their decision, implementing it and communicating about it; and subsequently to put it into practice. Many found this a practical approach to a subject which before had seemed theoretical or general.

Taking each part of the complete decision cycle, let's look at the kind of judgements our bankers were having to make as they redesigned the way they approached making, executing and communicating their decisions.

STEP 1

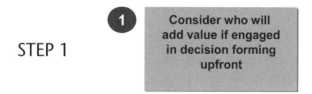

1 — Consider who will add value if engaged in decision forming upfront

The beginning of any decision-making process is usually marked by a crisis, managing a planning process or routine meeting, or the emergence of an opportunity. Each requires the leader to make a judgement, which may or may not be made easier if it is informed by more data or the inclusion of others in the decision-forming phase.

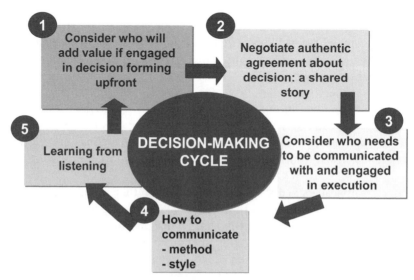

Figure 5.1   Decision-making cycle

Our investment bankers were largely split between the majority who made personal intuitive judgements on their own and those who canvassed opinion and sought more data.

Their judgements were largely instinctive rather than considered. But when asked to make a rational judgement between approaches to engagement and encouraged to weigh the benefits, costs and risks of each approach, they all modified their instinctive choice.

Whilst these individuals could see rationally that inclusion of others at the outset of their decision process might add value to both the content of the decision and its acceptability, they were concerned too about slowing things down.

Those with reservations about speed can sometimes be dealt with by asking them to recall the life cycle of other decisions where the appearance of speed at the front end was often subverted during implementation by those who held unsought views.

Key learning from Step 1

- Involving is only good if it adds value and creates more ownership.

- Many issues require an instruction but some will not stick without involvement.

- Involvement takes time and good facilitation.

STEP 2

Negotiate authentic agreement about decision: a shared story

I expect you have been in many meetings where agreement seems to have been reached and the leader is so pleased that the decision is assumed to represent a lasting settlement and the group moves. Little or no attempt is made to check for understanding around the group.

Reflect for a moment on the basis for a robust peace treaty. No negotiator allows the negotiating parties to leave the room when the spirit of agreement is reached: the parties are required to negotiate over the precise wording of the agreement and to agree what they will be communicating to their stakeholders or supporters. It is then that participants are forced to reveal to themselves, and to others, the script that has formed in their heads. By sharing it with each other it becomes possible to see where there is agreement, confusion and outright disagreement enabling negotiations on the issues of substance to restart.

This illustrates how planning the communication as an integral part of decision making serves as a device both to conclude the decision and to reach a common approach to engaging those outside the negotiations. It also allows the leader or facilitator to keep control of the group before they disperse.

Going back to our bankers, in one meeting with a boss and his colleagues I asked the group of 18 to write down their perception of the department's strategy on their own. The leader protested that it was a waste of time as he had told them repeatedly what the strategy was.

When each revealed their personal scripts there were 18 different stories which reflected the stories they were sharing in the daily performances with their own people. The leader was amazed but reflected that a tell approach to strategy, no matter how many times you rammed it down people's throats it rarely gets internalized beyond the repetition of blandishments, not necessarily because people disagree but because telling and selling is an ineffective way to engage.

The most effective story-tellers are also good at editing their stories on their feet having gauged the interest of their audience – a useful skill.

Key learning from Step 2

- Most decision discussions stop at the spirit of agreement.

- The devil is in the detail of the scripts in each persons head.

- The content of the decision is not complete until personal scripts are shared and negotiated.

- Learn the art of editing (levels of content):

    – What is the tabloid newspaper headline for your story?

    – What is the 30-second elevator script?

    – What is the 15-minute discourse?

STEP 3

3 Consider who needs to be communicated with and engaged in execution

At this point in the decision-making cycle we have reached agreement and shared a common story. Now we need to consider who needs to be engaged in the implementation and, beyond that, who needs to be communicated with because they are in some way affected by it.

Understanding the demographics is key. Even if the population to be affected is known and small, knowing what influences those involved is key. If the population is large, diverse and multi-cultural, the demographics are crucial.

And most organisations are poor at internal demographics. They may know what influences customer buying patterns but generally have little data on their own people. Doing employee satisfaction surveys is not the answer. These may tell us about likes and dislikes but not about what influences opinions and decisions. Organisations need to be able to segment their populations by culture and to understand what influences the thinking of different groups, taking care to see this exercise as one which allows for better relationships rather than better manipulation. It is a fine line to be drawn!

Returning to our bankers, on reaching this step they need to consider the nine factors which will influence the success of their communication efforts:

- the contentiousness of the issue, decision or topic;

- cultural differences which result in different styles of response;

- history of the relationship;

- timing and setting;

- the power relations between the parties;

- what else is going on at the same time;

- the nature and clarity of the invitation to influence the decision, issue or topic;

- appropriateness of the tone of communication;

- underlying values and beliefs which dispose people to engage in different ways.

Let's look at these factors from the perspective setting to highlight the emotional context that most communication takes place in, but is rarely acknowledged, at least at work.

The everyday story of Jack and Jill. Jack comes home with a special surprise for Jill. He is the earning partner in the relationship and has taken it upon himself to book a rather exclusive holiday for them both in the Caribbean. He arrives home to find his partner with her best friend discussing the compromises which a new baby in the family means. And wishing to brighten the atmosphere announces the holiday plan. A moments silence is quickly replaced by the hasty departure of Jill's best friend and the recriminatory conversation which follows. The holiday exchange around the factors turns out to be typical of the pattern of misunderstandings between them:

- The nature and degree of the *contentiousness of the content* of the exchange. In Jack's case he probably knew that trying to wrap it up as a surprise would do little to hide his preference for the Caribbean over Jill's admittedly *sotto voce* preferences for a cheaper holiday and some new clothes for the child.

- *Cultural differences which result in different styles of response.* Jill is actually Chinese and has a slight preference to defer to her partner upon whom she has recently become financially dependent. She may be much more understated than him but she expects him to 'read' her and be sensitive to this difference without the need for occasional verbal punch-ups when he goes too far.

- The *history of the relationship* and the recurring patterns which characterise it will provide a good predictor of how participants will react. Jack knew what was coming but was caught in the pattern before he could stop himself.

- *Timing and setting* are also critical determinants of the outcome of the engagement. We all know that the sequence in which who hears what from whom, matters to those on the receiving end.

- The *power relations between the parties.* Power derives from a number of sources. Power belongs to those who have control over resources, those who can influence careers, those who have perceived status or expertise, those who have community or political clout or plain old physical strength. In organisational settings there is power derived from association with powerful people, so-called 'referent power'. Jill's new dependency is certainly at play in the vignette.

- *What else is going on at the same time* will also influence the other party's concentration and inclination to engage, even if they heartily wish to. Noise in the system is therefore another powerful factor which can serve to put your communication off the agenda or associate it with another topic. How often do we hear an executive team say 'of course they've been told, we put a communication out' or 'we did a road show' forgetting that there was a redundancy process at the time and no one was in a ready state to engage.

- There is also the question of *what invitation to shape the decision* is inherent in the communication from one party to another. Is this an instruction, an invitation to think it over and debate, a chance to go off and be empowered? Or what exactly? Most organisational communication shows little sign of this being thought through.

- The *appropriateness of tone.* Perhaps more than any other factor this is the one which makes the greatest impact on how you and I and everyone else reacts and participates in a conversation or a more corporate effort to engage us.

With so many factors affecting a simple communication it is little wonder that it can go horribly wrong. The simple point is that beyond operational instructions there no such thing as a purely transactional, rational communication either at home or in the workplace. Most exchanges between people are emotionally and politically charged and affected by the same factors which surround Jack and Jill's discussion.

My conclusion is that we must remember that a communication is nearly always set in the context of a relationship between individuals or entities.

Key learning from Step 3

- Communication is set in the context of a relationship.

- Few communications can be purely transactional because of the emotional history.

- The relationship has to be considered as well as the message/content or task to hand.

STEP 4 **How to communicate - method - style**

Method

The methods or channels are the most visible part of the communication process. They are where some leaders consider communication starts and stops. But of course they are simply the manifestation of the planning stages outlined in the steps above or, in their absence, of a leader's instincts.

But before we get too carried away with methods and processes it's worth recalling that most communication by most leaders is informal and done on the fly. Table 5.1 invites readers to consider what their default modes of communicating are. Imagine you asked your direct reports to characterise your preferred way of communicating with them. How would they allocate 100 points around the options below?

Table 5.1   Default modes of communication

Mode	Method	%
See (push)	• email • paper	?
Hear (dialogue)	• voicemail • meetings	?
Experiences (creative interactions)	• learning experiences • workshop • brainstorm • workouts	?

Key learning from Step 4: Method

- Be clear about the outcome required.

- Match the method to the outcome.

Sources: Getty Images (John Prescott) and Photolibrary Group (Boris Yeltsin)

Style

Bosses get labelled with soubriquets such as 'Boxcar Willie' Walsh (British Airway's CEO), 'Fred the Shred' (Fred Goodwin of Royal Bank of Scotland) and 'Neutron Jack' (Jack Welch, ex-CEO of General Electric). And we all remember iconic moments which define our perceptions of a leader and which often become the stuff of legend and myth. They may be personal memories of intimate moments or stories writ large across the organisation. Both can get written into folklore. I have a few of my own.

During a spell as Bechtel's first European Head of Corporate Communication I had to fetch George Shultz from presenting on stage to clients to take a call from the White House which later resulted in him joining the Reagan cabinet.

Whilst at Marathon Oil, based in the American mid west, I found myself transferring from a scheduled jumbo jet at New York onto a company jet. It was icy under foot and I found the jet all locked up with the lights on but no obvious front door bell. I hammered on the fuselage and the ramp whirred open revealing the only other passenger, the CEO. I thought, what am I going to say to him for the next three hours or so? But I needn't have worried. He told me to sit down; he was going to be barman for the trip, the deal being we'd talk about everything but not after the flight. That did a young executive's ego a power of memorable good!

Like politicians, leaders have those moments where they steal the stage or are brought down by it. Ask any group of managers who makes a good communicator; many will cite a hero business figure or sportsperson. Good communication is often still seen to be limited to presentational skill and presence.

But it is the less iconic moments which craft a leader's reputation: it is the day-to-day performances which leaders give, almost unaware of their cumulative impact.

Leaders ascend from working in small pools of colleagues where communication is firmly set in the context of relationships, to a place above, usually physically and hierarchically, where they are removed from those they direct. Having made their ascent they soon adopt rituals for communicating with their people: probably a combination of one-to-ones, formal start-the-week meetings, informal lunches, drop-ins, town hall meetings and the like. And soon enough the participants will become familiar with the patterns which each of these takes and what behaviour they need to adopt to survive and thrive in them.

During these interactions the leader will adopt a small number of different styles, typically three or four, which characterise their performances. Usually unwittingly the leader conducts the communication as a character actor playing ever-so-predictable styles. We know from interviewing hundreds of employees that leaders do this.

We also know that few leaders have much awareness about the combination of styles they are known for, loved for and hated for. As in any soap the performance is more mesmerizing or tedious than the underlying story or business to conduct. Effective leaders are more aware of their styles and how to flex them for the situation to hand.

Good communicators are not born they are made. Once an individual realises that what lies between them achieving their aims is their ability to engage their people, they will want to learn from those who see it as a capability to be learnt and practiced.

Readers may wish to review the communication styles in Table 5.2 and judge which three or four their colleagues and staff might attribute to them.

Key learning from Step 4: Style

- Most of us have a number of communication styles which we adopt.

- Our style can help or hinder the outcome of the communication/ engagement.

- Different situations call for different styles.

Table 5.2   Communication styles

Style	Language	Tone	Body language
EXPERT/ TEACHER	precise, repetitive, checking stories, fables	authority, expert focus on transfer of knowledge, energetic	movement, engaging everyone, eye contact
EVANGELIST	positive, jokes, humour	upbeat, excited, sound bites, passion, loud, high energy, quite short bursts	expansive
ONE OF THE GANG	jargon of audience, street humour	irreverent, conspiring, low-key, personal, cult	reflecting audience
MAVERICK	challenge, create new jargon, optional/joker	cocky, irreverent	not reflecting the target of change
CONFIDANT	agreement, secrecy, security, assurance, empathy rather than humour	confessional, neutral, reflecting audience	reassuring
ARBITER	simple	even, firm, unexcitable, measured	two handed, equal attention
TEASE/ FLIRT	flattering, personal, humour	light	coquettish
LOBBYISTS	expert words jargon, confidential, self-confident	pressing, firm, melodious	attention keeping
BULLY	direct	clipped, terminal	emphatic
SNIPER	gotcha!	smug	still until ambush
VISIONARY	value-laden, well-chosen, well-versed, imagery, metaphor	conviction	presidential
TEAM COACH	accessible, collaborative, story telling	friendly but slightly distant, confident	openness, embracing
REPORTER	straightforward, unambiguous, factual	credibility without ownership of the issues	statuesque, slow motion
AUTOCRAT	clipped, no humour	aloof, dismissive, sweeping	

Source: John Smythe/Smythe Dorward Lambert

STEP 5

5

Learning from listening

I do not mean to give the impression that listening takes place only at one juncture: far from it, the good communicator is sensing, testing and inviting challenge throughout. Indeed the first step requires the good communicator to consider who to invite into the process before the die is cast on the decision.

But towards the end of the implementation process it is good to be able to make sense of the impact of the decision or change process in terms of what people now think, what they feel and what actions have resulted and what behaviours are being exhibited and experienced.

Listening is of course both a personal practice and a process to get wider, more formal input.

As a personal practice there is something of a rule of thumb that as we get more powerful our mouths get bigger and our ears smaller!

Source: Istockphoto/Beat Glauser

What are the attributes of the good listener? Good listening is less to do with how much we hear and more to do with why we are listening. In other words the quality of listening is governed by our motivation to listen. I believe that there are many motivations to listen:

To persuade: I listen to check what you know and persuade you of my view.

To defend: I listen in order to defend my position by seeking hooks in your dialogue on which to base the defence or furthering of my position.

- *To attack*: I listen, as a barrister might, to determine the fault that lies in your argument and counter-attack as soon as I sense an opportunity to overwhelm you.

- *To negotiate common cause*: I listen to seek out platforms for common agreement.

- *To appreciate*: I listen to appreciate your ideas and contributions.

- *To care*: I listen to understand and care for you.

- *To have fun*: I listen to introduce humour.

Most of us are pretty savvy about knowing what kind of listening is being employed by our boss; the history of the relationship usually throws up the clues. Once alerted to the mode of listening adopted we decide whether to be open or elliptical. Bosses who gain a reputation for listening to manipulate soon cut themselves off from their people.

Most people are able to spot the rhino trying to disguise himself as a wise owl.

As to the formal processes of listening, the same fundamental question arises: what is the motivation for listening? Is it to see what has been understood in order to renew the communication process or is it more about a dialogue?

Those embarking on a formal process of listening need to understand what the organisation's motivation is – to listen or obtain feedback.

Key learning from Step 5

- Be aware of your motivation for listening; is it to engage or to manipulate?

- Try and be aware of what permissions you need to give to your audience before they will engage authentically with you. What does your track record with them tell you about your credibility with them?

- What is the organisation's track record on listening; is there positive action after employee surveys and the like, or are they tick-box palliatives or outright charades?

6 Measuring Employee Satisfaction is a Waste of Time

DRIVERS OF EMPLOYEE ENGAGEMENT

There is widespread use of the word 'driver' in the lexicon of employee research and measurement. I don't particularly like the jargon, but rather than fight it let's explain it.

A 'driver' is a source of influence on employees which results in them thinking, feeling and behaving differently. Thus the thinking goes that if you can pin down the influences or drivers which result in changes to understanding and behaviour it will be possible to manage the sources of influence and bring about broad-scale changes to the way people think, feel and behave. Whether this is an ethical or productive endeavour is controversial.

Types of driver or influence on people include:

- *behaviours* – particularly of immediate bosses, the role models of distant bosses and the behaviour of other influential figures;

- *experiences* – perhaps key meetings, learning events, periods of change;

- *benefits* – such as pay, conditions of employment and so on.

Any or all of these may influence employees to think, feel and behave differently.

Experts will debate which drivers may improve a group's performance or which may accelerate the adoption of a change process. The assumption is that if you can understand the drivers which influence people positively you should be able to enhance the positive ones and dilute the negative drivers.

It is a grand assumption.

ETHICS AND USEFULNESS OF LARGE-SCALE EMPLOYEE RESEARCH

It is also very difficult to make hard and fast correlations between cause and effect. The behaviours of an individual or a group are hard to explain. It is also a rather sinister assumption in that it suggests that it is possible and legitimate for management to understand what drives the 'rat in their cage' and stimulate the behaviours by altering the drivers.

Indeed the ethics and desirability of attempting to coerce and stimulate the right behaviours are hinted at throughout this book. I am of the view that attempts to coerce people to think, feel and behave in ways pre-ordained by an elite, aside from being distasteful, are unlikely to bring the best out of people.

To bring the best out of people I contend that management should no longer view the company as a vehicle which owns its human assets but instead should see their people as being on temporary loan during which they can benefit from their creativity provided people feel invited to participate.

By nature I am ambivalent about much of employee measurement. In many large organisations it has taken on the appearance of an end in itself involving employees in yet more bureaucratic activity for remote corporate centres who kid themselves into thinking that they are listening to employees.

It is certainly the case that the desire to understand what influences what people think, how they feel and how they behave has spawned an entire measurement and research supply industry.

Few big companies do without some sort of employee survey process. Some employees are subjected to so much research that they will groan and reflect their irritation in their responses; as will layers of middle management when the HR department directs them to get involved in 'post-survey action processes'.

I have a suspicion that the survey epidemic is peaking and that there is a move towards much simpler, more targeted and less bureaucratic ways of taking the pulse of the people. Fast intranet technology is already enabling this change. Plus I predict that the corporate world will increasingly borrow from the political world and do less grand-scale measures of general employee satisfaction and much more specific-issue research.

In any event this chapter is based on the assumption that people like to measure their investments to see if they are getting promised benefits and to see what people are thinking and feeling.

I am in favour of highly focused measurement exercises which can be used as a genuine lever to get management to pause and connect with employees. So much of it is of the once-a-year variety of multi-question inquisition which produces vast amounts of indigestible data.

In this chapter I ask you to challenge what is actually being measured and whether in fact much change occurs as a result. I admit I am a reluctant measurer.

Why? It is said, too often, that what gets measured gets done. I'm not so sure that the cumbersome research and so-called action processes so many of us have endured in large organisations are anything more than a knee-jerk purchase based on promise of higher performance of benchmarked companies.

I would hazard a guess that most apparent links between benchmarked measures of employee satisfaction and business performance are accidental.

DUBIOUS VALUE OF BENCHMARKING

That said, I am a believer in smaller-scale research when it is directly designed to assist a change process, improve day-to-day business performance or to identify and test the unique drivers of engagement in the organisation.

I am very dubious about benchmarking employee engagement between organisations. Benchmarking seems to appeal most to competitive leaders who are more concerned with their own vanity than the needs and drivers of their people. Every organisation I have ever consulted with has protested its uniqueness and for the most part resisted off-the-shelf solutions; yet when it comes to employee research and measurement, many follow the crowd.

Why? The accepted wisdom is that if we can identify the best solutions and practices out there we can learn more quickly than if we had to invent them ourselves. So far, so good. Benchmarking solutions and practices may be a useful thing to do. But most employee research benchmarking sheds little light on solutions and practices. For the most part it compares how people score their companies on the drivers being measured; and mostly these are measures of employee satisfaction.

I accept that comparisons may act as a spur to leaders to do things better and that is useful, but I think that too often the comparisons are little more than a vanity exercise and often an apparently good score results in complacency.

I have sat through many presentations of the results of benchmarked employee research which feature numbers which purport to show that our people are 'more satisfied' than those of benchmarked companies; and that these have resulted in slightly higher customer satisfaction scores. Here lies the trap: in doing somewhat better we create complacency justified by the benchmark.

This is the point when a category-busting start-up rips up the rule book and outstrips the established order.

Organisations start to see the top benchmark scores as a glass ceiling as opposed to a challenge. My first objection, in summary, is that benchmarking will show how people are scoring their companies but throws little light on why this is the case.

IDENTIFY THE INFLUENCES OR DRIVERS OF EMPLOYEE ENGAGEMENT UNIQUE TO YOUR ORGANISATION AND SITUATION

My second objection to benchmarking is the danger that benchmarking results in isomorphism or convergence of strategy, brand and employee experience; they do it, so will we. Companies spend millions identifying a unique positioning or brand to differentiate themselves in their markets and then strive to do the opposite by paying to much attention to the practices of competitors and benchmarks.

To do so is the hallmark of follower rather than leader. If that is the company's strategy, then it is a rational choice – if an EasyJet wanted to copy a Southwest Airlines for example.

I contend that organisations should identify the drivers of engagement which are peculiar to them and trust their instincts by shaping the experience of work around them.

We observe that there are three common categories of influences or drivers which may contribute to heightened engagement. They are:

- instrumental drivers
    - pay
    - benefits
- cultural drivers
    - values
    - ethics
    - reputation/standing
    - community contribution

- brand

- business vision/purpose/mission and strategy

- leadership example from symbolic leaders

- workplace drivers

  - right level of challenge; opportunities to apply my creativity

  - work I want to do

  - bosses who engage me appropriately in decision making/ change

  - bosses who are fair

  - bosses who inspire me

  - bosses who give me the opportunity and resources to develop my capabilities

  - bosses who stretch, trust and make me accountable

  - colleagues who I respect, like and learn from.

But more of identifying and measuring drivers of engagement later, for now I would like to look back at and challenge the old concept of employee satisfaction and suggest that it is time to challenge it as the desired state that we wish to achieve in our organisations.

ARE SATISFIED EMPLOYEES GOOD FOR BUSINESS?

If we step back and look at the cultural impact of researching people, what do we see?

Put yourself in the shoes of the employee of a big company (or maybe just look down!) faced with responding to a survey seeking to elicit your views about the work experience.

To many it is just another chore to be completed. To some it is a chance to mouth off about specific or general irritations.

Typically it will ask you to rate your satisfaction with a long list of factors said to be the drivers of satisfaction of employees with their work. Typically these include:

- remuneration and benefits

- physical working conditions

- content of job

- career development

- relationship with bosses

- organisational communication

- social activities

- comfort with representing the organisation/brand

- and often much, much more!

The key phrase for the last 20 years has been employee satisfaction.

Companies fall over themselves to attract and retain people and the survey industry has been built on the contention that the satisfaction of employees is a good thing because it is contended that satisfied employees reciprocate with loyalty (retention) and high performance.

BUSINESS AND CULTURAL CONSEQUENCES OF ENCOURAGING AND MEASURING EMPLOYEE SATISFACTION

Do we really want satisfied employees? Do we really want retention?

Think of the roots of the word 'satisfy': 'meeting the expectation of desires' (Oxford English Dictionary). The implication is that organisations choose to meet the expectations of the desires of their people. This can mean the endless provision or fulfilment of those drivers which are deemed to satisfy people and in turn result in them being retained and performing better.

The real question we need to ask ourselves when we embark on or review employee measurement and research is: *What is the business and cultural outcomes we are hoping to encourage by the measurement process?*

Too often the motivations for internal research are copy-cat. Other companies do it so we ought to.

I believe that there may be unintended outcomes from measuring and pursuing employee satisfaction. One is employee retention. Is employee retention necessarily good for business? Another is creating higher and higher expectations of being satisfied by the company. When the time then comes to change the organisation people see their view of the psychological contract, reinforced annually by 'the survey', being torn up.

Satisfied employees who have had all their desires sated are likely to be a fairly sleepy lot. Many a time have I consulted with large organisations where the inmates seem almost smugly satisfied with the easy life which their employers have heaped on them. Being satisfied makes them unprepared for harder times.

Measuring satisfaction often results in rigorous attempts to raise their satisfaction scores by topping up the drivers which fall short. Naturally the employees sense that all they need to do is to keep saying 'we're not satisfied'; and they never are of course. Just like children if you ask them if they need more sweets the answer will rarely be no.

The central problem with measuring employee satisfaction is that everything about the psychological contract (between employer and employee) has changed.

Retaining employees from cradle to grave was the assumption underpinning the received wisdom that achieving employee satisfaction was good for business. It is no longer the case and so what we measure, if we must measure at all, must change.

Figure 6.1 is a reminder of the key shifts which have been taking place in the psychological contract between employer and employee.

Whilst there are many institutions which can still claim that they have not and may even not wish to see these shifts in the psychological contract, particularly in the public sector, most organisations are living with a fundamental change in relationship with their employees.

Yet most are still making the assumption that employee satisfaction is a goal worth chasing and measuring. Employees are now less concerned with being retained and less impressed with the culture of employee satisfaction which was fostered to preserve the old loyalty-based cradle-to-grave psychological contract.

Cradle to grave	portfolio careers
Loyalty	transactional relationship
Dependence	independence
'Our human resources'	creative talent on loan
Employees	citizens
Big institutions	my own company
Command and control	well-governed inclusivity
CEO = GOD	CEO = Guide
I left the company	I left my boss
Local community	workplace communities

Figure 6.1   Seismic shifts in the psychological contract

Employees are now concerned about different types of drivers which influence what they think, feel and how they behave:

- employability – they want to build their technical, leadership and managerial capabilities so that they can advance themselves and choose who they work for;

- values, ethics and conduct of employers;

- bosses and a culture which encourages them to participate appropriately and creatively in the decision making which affects their work;

- work–life balance.

Measuring and developing employee satisfaction reinforces the command-and-control culture

Measuring and developing employee satisfaction is counterproductive because it reinforces the command-and-control leadership model. It does so by casting employees as passive spectators and reinforces their role as evaluators of the rewards offered by the employer for their loyalty and compliance, neither of which do employees wish to offer within a culture of command and control. They are voting against it by leaving.

New-look employee satisfaction research may make passing nods to stimulating 'feedback' and encouraging people to 'feel involved' but fundamentally these are presentational sinecures to make organisations look progressive. Beneath them lie the remnants of the old psychological contract referred to in the diagram above.

So if we accept that we do not want to perpetuate command and control as the pervasive default culture, what measurement should we be undertaking in order to encourage the drivers which bring the best out of our people?

WHAT, HOW AND HOW OFTEN SHOULD YOU CONSIDER MEASURING?

In reviewing your employee research it will be worth keeping three tests in mind. I have expressed them as questions:

- What are the business and cultural outcomes we are hoping to encourage by the measurement process? Are these outcomes ethical and productive?

- Have we designed a research process which results in us asking questions which really will tell us if our people are being engaged or are we still only measuring satisfaction?

- Have we aligned our customer and employee research programmes?

That said, let's look at the three types of employee research which I believe can add value to the business and to the employee and customer experience:

- understanding the demographics of the organisation and how they influence the relationship and communication between employees and employer;

- identifying and measuring the key drivers which have the greatest influence on the performance and affiliation of your people;

- tracking and adapting change and transformation.

UNDERSTANDING THE DEMOGRAPHICS OF THE ORGANISATION

However large or small your organisation you can view it as a community which is shaped by the demographics of its inhabitants. The demographics will be in constant flux. In the first era of internal communication people felt that they owed their loyalty to the organisation and would, by and large, listen and engage with efforts by the organisation to include them in dialogue. Little attempt was made to understand the demographics of the workforce and communication, particularly of the formal corporate kind, tended to be of the one-size-fits-all variety.

A reasonable understanding of the demographics enables managers to adapt to the groups and avoid howlers.

A simple addition to existing research or an occasional enquiry should be made to understand:

- the community backgrounds of their employees and what those backgrounds mean in terms of how people are disposed to react and behave;

- what different groups want from work; and what is their idea of the tacit contract that exists between employee and employer;

- what people read, watch, listen to outside work;

- which sources of influence are credible and why (for example peers, bosses, unions, community leaders, other companies);

- insights into the credibility and faith people have in the communication and engagement practices of their own bosses;

- the credibility and faith people have in the formal and informal communication processes and networks in the company.

Aside from formal research processes, organisations can consider the creation of a culture or demographics panel to advise how different groups may react to change and communication and on how to encourage involvement in change. Although care must also be taken to avoid the misuse of demographics, provided the motivation is to improve the relationship and connection between employer and employee, all will be well. If it becomes more about manipulating opinion, it will backfire.

IDENTIFYING AND MEASURING THE KEY DRIVERS WHICH HAVE THE GREATEST INFLUENCE ON THE PERFORMANCE AND AFFILIATION OF YOUR PEOPLE

Earlier I asserted that measuring employee satisfaction served to reinforce the old contract in which the employer provides security in exchange for relatively unquestioning loyalty. In my view it also reinforces the parent/child relationship in which the employer, as parent, is chasing the expectations of employees, expectations which it has set through the employee satisfaction process.

In this sense the old contract is peculiarly set in favour of the employee; all the employer was asking for was loyalty and compliance.

Today the employer cannot offer security and should not be seeking to encourage compliance and unquestioning loyalty.

Conversely the employer should be creating an experience of work in which the employee wants to volunteer their creativity and constructive challenge. The measures of engagement ought to be in the assessment of the disposition by employees to act, take risk and challenge (as well as some elements of instrumental satisfaction like reward, which must be competitive).

There ought to be a better balance between the employee's agenda and the employer's agenda. In the new deal the employee should be encouraged to volunteer their creativity in exchange for personal development and work experience which improves their chances of advancement in the firm and their employability beyond their current employer.

Figure 6.2 illustrates the shift from measuring employee satisfaction to measuring other drivers which will result in more engaged employees. Readers might want to reflect where the balance of their measurement lies. Is it more on the left side than the right? In reflecting you might also consider carefully the actual questions you are asking.

I have listened to many people who say that they are measuring drivers of engagement but on probing what specific questions are being asked it becomes clear that they are often measuring whether people feel involved in decision making, as opposed to asking them if they have explicitly been invited to join the decision-making or change process.

What's wrong with that? Feeling involved is OK. But it does not tell us if employees have the opportunity in the course of routine business and change to contribute their ideas. It does not tell us if the power balance has shifted, which it must if the organisation is attempting to change the culture from 'decide and tell/sell' to one where risks are routinely taken to engage the right groups in decision making and change.

Alternative route to identifying and tracking drivers of engagement

The alternative route has five core steps:

1. What are the (ethically acceptable) business and cultural outcomes we are hoping to encourage by the measurement process?

2. Identifying existing pockets of effective engagement yielding business/cultural outcomes.

3. Identifying the key drivers of engagement which had the most impact on performance and 'happiness' with the job.

4. Tracking the drivers; deciding what to ask and how often.

5. 'Not another process': using measurement to drive performance.

1. What are the business and cultural outcomes we are hoping to encourage by the measurement process?

No measurement can begin without putting the exercise in the context of the organisation's situation. Is it in crisis, strategic complacency or transformation?

Satisfaction with	Personal implication
• Pay, conditions, environment • Work experience • Relationships • Career • Leadership • Communication	• Opportunity to participate in decision making • Degree of discretionary effort • Readiness to take risk • Collaboration beyond work team • Ownership of change • Desire to stay based on appetite for improvement
Passive spectators	Personally committed reformer

Figure 6.2   What do you measure?

I noted earlier that the real question we need to ask ourselves when we embark on or review employee measurement and research is: 'What are the business and cultural outcomes we are hoping to encourage by the measurement process?'

Thus the first step in any review must be to engage the right people in responding to this question. Who are the right people to do this? I do not consider that the group should be confined to functional departments like HR and communication. If it is the case that what gets measured gets done, great care should be taken in deciding what to measure, because the measures, if acted on, will change the culture of the organisation.

The options are:

- Ask the same questions that every other organisation is being asked in a benchmark survey. I have already said why I think that this is the wrong road to take, but if it is the choice you have made, consider also asking some questions which are unique to your organisation.

- Get top management to consider what drivers they want to measure and encourage. Making it elitist at least gets top management involved but it does mean that you are likely to restrict the measures which top management are keenest on and fail to listen to what others have to say.

- Get the functional specialists to decide. I do not favour this route as it frames the exercise as a functional process rather than a business priority.

- Engage a broader population; not surprisingly my favoured route because it delivers a balance of drivers and creates broader ownership.

In one global company, engaging a broader group meant giving the work of narrowing down the measures to a number of different groups of staff and managers. Each was given the same briefing about the strategic challenge – in this case to grow market share or be swallowed.

Each had to paint a picture of the kind of culture which would help support the business strategy and each had to agree a definition of engagement and the key engagement drivers which they thought might provide a stimulating environment for staff and one which would help the business achieve its business aim.

Common definitions were agreed and negotiations were made visible via the intranet and other communication channels. One of the teams was the executive group who felt that opening up the definition stage had contributed to creating a common goal for the measurement process.

2. Identifying existing pockets of effective engagement

Whilst step 1 was underway, step 2 had already started. In a joint initiative between communication, human resources and commercial, executives had identified high- and low-performing teams, locations, business units, departments and even particular work shifts.

Interviews were conducted by some members of the original task force among selected groups from high- and low-performing groups, in which links were sought between higher and lower business performance and their relationship with the key drivers of engagement. Most attention was paid to the everyday engagement practices of the immediate leader, manager or supervisor in question – the work experience drivers.

3. Identifying the key drivers of engagement which had the most impact on performance and happiness with the job

Task force members regrouped and were given the challenge of determining the relationships between high and low performance and the engagement practices of leaders, managers and supervisors. They also had to agree a weighting of the importance of the other two key categories of employee engagement. All three categories of driver are repeated here for ease of reference:

- instrumental drivers
  - pay
  - benefits
- cultural drivers (degree of alignment with and more importantly consent to)
  - values
  - ethics
  - reputation/standing
  - community contribution
  - brand
  - business vision/purpose/mission and strategy
  - leadership example from symbolic leaders
- workplace drivers
  - right level of challenge; opportunities to apply my creativity
  - work I want to do
  - bosses who engage me appropriately in decision making/ change

- bosses who are fair
- bosses who inspire me
- bosses who give me the opportunity and resources to develop my capabilities
- bosses who stretch, trust and make me accountable
- colleagues who I respect, like and learn from.

4. Tracking the drivers; deciding what to ask and how often

The answer to the 'how often' question is answered by deciding who needs to be listening to the results and taking action on them. In post-merger integration I recommend that a small but organisation-wide representative sample be taken monthly, with hot spots included where it is key to track changing mood. The post-merger integration group will usually be hungry for data.

For general tracking of levels of employee engagement the period ought to be tied to key milestones in the strategy or planning cycle. Highly operational businesses will often have a 90-day or quarterly cycle in which the previous period business targets are reviewed and next quarters are set. These occasions are a good time to focus attention on the people and what is or is not driving them.

Deciding what specific questions to ask will be become clear from the analysis of the relationships between good business performance and engagement drivers which are reported to contribute to business performance.

The boxes opposite contain some sample employee questions designed to tap levels of engagement; input may be qualitative or quantitative.

5. 'Not another process': using measurement to drive performance.

I complained earlier about over-sized bureaucratic post-research action processes. But of course there must be an action process. The essence of the alternate approach described above is to help leaders of identifiable units, departments and so on to understand the link between business performance for their own area and the drivers of engagement over which they have some or complete influence. All leaders, managers and supervisors have responsibility for the workplace drivers.

They should be motivated to understand the results for their part of the organisation, however small it is, and to take their share of the responsibility for the drivers of engagement within their teams. But it is not just the boss who is responsible for the workplace drivers. Everyone is a contributor to the quality of life in their team. So the emphasis of the post-measurement

1. What engagement is like in our organisation

Are people personally implicated?

- I have freedom to develop ideas
- I have responsibility to drive things forward
- I feel stretched/challenged at work
- I am trusted to get on with it
- I have a sense of ownership for what I am working on

Discretionary effort

- I see the difference my work makes
- I believe the difference is valuable
- I am ready to do more than is expected of me – to go the extra mile
- I can honestly say that I am truly committed to my work and what we are all trying to achieve

Engagement approach

- I understand the need to change/enhance day-to-day performance
- I understand because I have been told
- I understand because I have worked it out for myself
- I have the opportunity to influence how things are done where I work
- I feel I generally do what others have determined I should do, not what I think should be done
- The reality of our engagement experience is true to the promise

Determining the engagement approach (questions for senior management)

- We actively consider the type of engagement we want and what we will need to do to enable such an approach to succeed
- Our approach to engagement is not considered, it is impulsive
- I actively modify my behaviour to enable those around me to have a better engagement opportunity
- We invite people who will have to implement change or improvement to be instrumental in determining the change that is needed
- The reality of our engagement experience is true to the promise

2. Why it is like it is

Personal opportunity

- I am trusted
- I am stretched
- I am able to voice ideas
- My manager values my ideas
- My manager encourages ideas from others
- I am encouraged to take a journey into the unknown in order to find better ways of getting things done
- I feel a great sense of personal responsibility for my work
- I have sufficient opportunity to be creative/innovative

Change and transformation

- When new approaches are needed, generally
    - I am told what to do with little or no explanation as to why
    - Someone explains why and helps me understand what I need to do
    - I have the opportunity to explore why the change is needed and some scope to determine how what I need to do should be done
    - I am asked my views about how we could improve things, before any decisions are made

- The people responsible for making decisions that affect my work do not understand what I do

Motivation

- I believe in what we are all trying to achieve
- I come to work because I need a job
- I come to work because I enjoy what I do
- I come to work because I believe I am doing something important
- I am proud of what I do
- I am proud of who I work for
- My efforts are recognised by my boss

---

3. The difference it makes

Personal performance

- Which of these best describe the way you feel about your work

    - It energises me
    - I am interested in it
    - I believe it is important
    - It bores me
    - When I put in extra hours it is because I have so much to do that I need to create more time to finish it
    - When I put in extra hours it is because I am so engaged in my work that I want to progress it as far as possible

- I see the connection between my job and what the organisation is trying to achieve overall
- Leaders create opportunities for others to get engaged
- I am ready to do what is expected of me, but am not interested in going beyond that
- I am ready to go the extra mile and often do
- I am ready to go the extra mile but there are things happening elsewhere that prevent me from succeeding
- My boss understands the factors that are preventing people from going the extra mile

---

improvement process should not be framed as the manager's action list analysed and delivered by a grand committee, as it so often is with employee satisfaction surveys, but as accessible data which the whole team can take responsibility for analysing themselves.

And top management must still attend to taking action on the first two categories of drivers, the instrumental and cultural drivers which middle- and lower-level supervisors have little or no control over.

So now to the third and last type of measurement.

TRACKING AND ADAPTING CHANGE AND TRANSFORMATION

What's the difference between change and transformation? I think it is a matter of size, scale and ambition. A change process implies a transactional change to processes, procedures and systems which may be huge but does not require reworking every aspect of a company's make-up.

A transformation does mean just that – transforming everything. Figure 6.3 is a McKinsey and Company diagram which I had a hand in influencing when I spent time with them as an Organisational Fellow. The concept stresses the idea that transformation requires changes both to the visible processes and systems and to the less-visible DNA driving the organisation, like ambition, purpose and collective beliefs.

Regardless of whether it is change or transformation, both processes require those affected to give something up and to adopt something new. It involves loss and acceptance of new ways of thinking and behaving. Elsewhere in the book I argue that when imaginative ways of engaging people in change are

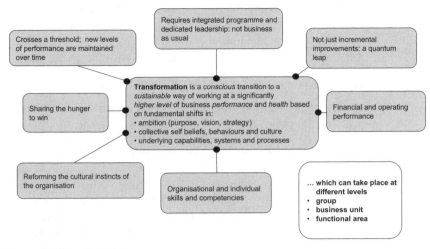

Source: McKinsey & Company

Figure 6.3   Transformation

used, people are far more likely to volunteer their support and feel ownership of the change.

Of course this just doesn't happen in many change processes or stops short with communication about the change, which we know from John Kotter's research, has little impact on people unless they are also engaged in the process. I also know from my consulting experience that cascading communication has little penetration. So there may be a process which the leadership thinks is getting the message over, but its impact is almost always overestimated.

One of the problems is that the sponsors and architects of change are immersed in it and somehow think that osmosis or telepathy will convey it to others.

Thus the utility of the change poll. These polls should be short and directed at gauging:

- understanding of the rationale for the change;

- understanding of the vision for the change and benefits which will be derived for the company, employees and other stakeholders;

- understanding of the process and the initiatives involved and how they all fit together;

- perceptions of belief in the programme held by employees and other groups;

- perceptions about the visibility and credibility of those leading it;

- levels of opposition and the reasons lying behind opposition (so that if they are simply mistaken they can be corrected, but if on the other hand they represent ideological or intellectual opposition, the holders of these views can be invited to debate them with the sponsors);

- particular concerns, need for information or reassurance;

- whether people feel that they are being adequately engaged in the process so that their ideas can contribute to the change;

- degree of excitement about the change/transformation.

Each research exercise needs to be tailored to the change being undertaken but a short measure based on the above would give a change team a pretty good pulse check and enable them to take action in response. It also provides the lead sponsor or CEO to zero in on specific parts of the change where things do not seem to be going well and to encourage leaders to take more visible ownership where this is seen to be lacking.

Questionnaires are not the only method available; Chapter 7 features other means of making the diagnostics a part of the change process.

I'll finish this chapter with an example of a change poll. This one is drawn from the case discussed in Chapter 10.

Poll on Transformation in Finance

Transformation: what transformation?

6. Are you aware that the Finance function is undergoing a transformation designed to radically improve its service to the business?

    Yes ☐ No ☐

7. Do you believe that the Finance function requires transformation?

(a) where you work

    Yes ☐ No ☐

(b) across the global finance function

    Yes ☐ No ☐

8. For each of the statements below, please indicate the extent to which you agree or disagree

		Strongly agree	Agree	Neither agree nor disagree	Disagree	Strongly disagree
a	I am aware of the business case or reasons for transforming the Finance function	☐	☐	☐	☐	☐
b	The transformation of Finance is urgent					
	i where I work	☐	☐	☐	☐	☐
	ii for the global Finance function	☐	☐	☐	☐	☐
c	I am familiar with the activities, initiatives and programmes being specifically implemented to implement transformation in Finance					
	i where I work	☐	☐	☐	☐	☐

		Strongly agree	Agree	Neither agree nor disagree	Disagree	Strongly disagree
	ii for the global Finance function	☐	☐	☐	☐	☐
d	The strategy driving the transformation is visible					
	i where I work	☐	☐	☐	☐	☐
	ii for the global Finance function	☐	☐	☐	☐	☐

Three shifts

There are three big shifts in our culture and approach to carrying out our duties which will help to transform our service offer. They are:

Transactional to analytical	Manual to automation	Complex to simple
We are shifting to a role that provides exceptional value and leadership to the company. Our emphasis will be on analysing and using our information for business advantage and higher profit.	We aim to streamline and automate much that is currently done manually. This will free up resources to focus on analysis and insight and enable us to build speed, greater accuracy and improved flexibility in all that we do.	Complexity kills our ability to be fast, focused and effective. We are driving simplicity through common approaches, centralised processes and effective support systems.

9.   Please indicate the extent to which you agree or disagree.

		Strongly agree	Agree	Neither agree nor disagree	Disagree	Strongly disagree
a	These shifts will help to transform Finance's service offer	☐	☐	☐	☐	☐
b	We are far advanced along the journey of moving from *transactional to analytical*					
	i where I work	☐	☐	☐	☐	☐
	ii for the global Finance function	☐	☐	☐	☐	☐

c   We are far advanced along the journey of moving from *manual to automation*

i where I work	☐	☐	☐	☐	☐
ii for the global Finance function	☐	☐	☐	☐	☐

d   We are far advanced along the journey of moving from *complex to simple*

i where I work	☐	☐	☐	☐	☐
ii for the global Finance function	☐	☐	☐	☐	☐

Becoming finance advisors to our business partners

As the shifts imply we aim to become business advisers to our internal partners…

10.   To what extent do you believe we have achieved our goal of becoming business advisers to our internal partners?

		Already there	Some work to do yet	Huge amount of work to do
a	in your place of work	☐	☐	☐
b	you personally	☐	☐	☐
c	globally across finance	☐	☐	☐

Visibility of the leadership in driving the transformation

11.   How visible is leadership in championing the transformation of Finance?

		Very visible	A little visible	Hardly visible	Not at all visible
a	where you work	☐	☐	☐	☐
b	globally across Finance	☐	☐	☐	☐

Effectiveness of communication about our transformation

12. How would you rate communication about the transformation of Finance?

		Very good	Good	Adequate	Poor	Very poor
a	where you work	☐	☐	☐	☐	☐
b	globally across Finance	☐	☐	☐	☐	☐

Your appetite to be more involved in transformation

13. For each of the following statements, please indicate the extent to which you agree or disagree.

		Strongly agree	Agree	Neither agree nor disagree	Disagree	Strongly disagree
a	I personally feel involved in the transformation	☐	☐	☐	☐	☐
b	I would like to be more involved in contributing to the transformation of Finance	☐	☐	☐	☐	☐

14. Finally, what one message would you like to give to the Finance leadership team about the transformation of Finance?

_____

_____

_____

_____

_____

_____

PART II

Designing and Implementing Effective Employee Engagement

7 Understanding Previous Habits of Engagement to Accelerate Change

Past behaviour is the best predictor of future behaviour according to Professor David Guest at Imperial College in London. From our research into employee engagement, the evidence suggests that repetitive patterns or habits build up in organisations in the way that employees are engaged at work.

Those patterns are of course reciprocal. The boss or the organisation behaves in a predictable fashion and the individual or group often responds in an equally predictable way.

This being the case, if you are planning a change, transformation or merger either on a grand scale or between small groups it pays to spend some time trying to understand how the groups have reacted to being engaged in a change process in the past. Doing so may enable the sponsor of change to disrupt or harness the existing patterns to accelerate the change.

The idea of creating sufficient turbulence to disrupt repetitive and probably compulsive patterns is not new. The idea is based on the experience that many have of managing change. Perfectly respectable plans are conceived and rationally explained to those being asked or required to change. One of three outcomes is likely:

- The saboteurs have no intention of complying and wear the sponsors down.

- The shell-shocked would like to comply but are too locked into old patterns and revert to previous patterns of behaviour.

- Cult members implement with fervour but little insight.

Turbulence wakes people and allows them to see the repetitive patterns which they are either voluntarily or involuntarily ensnared by. It provides them with a moment of clarity in which they can make personal choices about breaking the pattern or going with the flow – almost trance-like. It is this trance-like state which many of us as employees seem to live out parts of our corporate lives. In this state we make few conscious and personal decisions; we move with the synchronicity of a shoal of fish.

At times that is an answer to an angel's prayer. Sometimes the organisation needs its people to repeat processes and deliver service consistently.

UNDERSTANDING PREVIOUS PATTERNS OF ENGAGEMENT; GIVING THE WORK OF DIAGNOSIS TO THE PEOPLE AFFECTED

In times of large- or small-scale change, sponsors of the change need to ask themselves what response they are looking for. Do they want a compliant, trance-like response or do they want participants to have personal insight about their own stake and interest in the change? Which response to change is fit for purpose?

The programmatic, sheep-dip, change-by-road show and PowerPoint characterises most experiences employees have of change. But is there any evidence that a more personal, insight-based approach adds more value?

Anecdotally, yes. From our engagement research we can cite many organisations which attempted to understand the previous patterns of engagement and implicated their employees in the diagnostic process and through the collective insight gained created a readiness for the change as opposed to a weariness. Let's look at a few examples.

The logistics company

Its workforce was almost as disenfranchised as those in the freight company discussed in Chapter 3. They refused or could not see the case for change, having seen or experienced little of the competitive context themselves and sat as piggy in the middle between unions and employer in an endless exchange about the need or not for change.

In a moment of inspiration and realising that no amount of externally generated management-sponsored research or lecturing would persuade the workforce, the operations director sent very small groups of well-prepared workers to interview customers about the firm's service and delivery. Over a period of 3 months, stories of the dire straits the company was in, compared to competitors, began to circulate on the shop floor.

These stories were passed back by the interviewers not management. And the debate about the need for change began without management lifting another finger.

In another masterstroke the operations director asked the interviewers to pool their findings and analyses together and present first to their colleagues rather than management. The interviewers presented and argued the case for change as convincingly as any manager.

The sceptic may argue that the workers were being manipulated into doing their masters bidding. But the external research brief, whilst structured, drew no foregone conclusions. The worker researchers came to their own conclusions that there was a need for change. Of course they differed on solutions to the problem, but the exercise had created an openness to the need to develop a solution.

Taking a walk on the wild side

It is not just the shop floor who can be blockers to change! A major financial services company had for many years encouraged its business units to go their own way to encourage accountability for financial targets. Over time they became individually successful but the group fragmented into fiefdoms which found it hard to collaborate where it made commercial sense.

As lost opportunity and revenues became increasingly visible, an interesting initiative was embarked upon to bring the executives closer.

Rather than put people through a desk-based development process, the company sent their executives to work in non-corporate environments such as not-for-profit businesses and small entrepreneurial start-ups. The executives learnt what it was like to be stripped, albeit temporarily, of their positional or hierarchical power and having to rely on influencing skills to guide and participate. Some found themselves helping disabled children to learn.

This was not executive tourism: they had come to learn and to contribute. And the company has retained relationships with many of the organisations the executives visited. Indeed reciprocal visits were arranged.

The visits equipped the executives to deal with each other using influencing and listening skills which had been supplanted by politicking and power games. They spent a week together working through possibilities for the business which would require collaborative cross-business solutions. At the end of the week their proposals were put to the CEO and formed the basis for some future new business ventures.

Participants remarked that it had achieved results because it had surprised them and made it safe to step out from their corporate defences and take risks with colleagues, with whom to do so in the normal line of business would have been unthinkable. 'We would never have done that in a classroom learning environment. The trick for us is to take it back to our everyday relationships.'

Giving the business back to the bankers

A high street bank had for years run a successful operation from the centre. Most decisions had, in effect, been centralised. Like other banks they had made a god of sales and revenue and for a long time the formula worked. But the public has come to tire of a sales-based relationship with their bank. And miss-selling scandals cast a shadow over the model.

Under new leadership, discussions began about the future face of banking. In the UK, the online bank First Direct had enabled customers to visit their bank when they wanted to and others had started down the road of a needs-based approach in which banks segmented or divided their customers into groups according to their needs and serviced them with different levels of service, charging accordingly of course.

In this case the bank wanted to bring back much higher levels of service combined with a needs-based approach. But they knew that their senior management population fell into the third category of allegiance: 'cult members who implemented with fervour but little insight'. And that suddenly changing the tune from sell, sell, sell to a new philosophy would be confusing and likely to be stillborn without some intervention.

Thus senior managers were requested to go to their annual conference, which normally was an exercise in mobilisation. This time it was an experience with an entirely different tone. Upon arrival the hundreds of attendees walked through what at first looked like a hall of fame of big famous companies and naturally enough they expected theirs to figure. They were not to be disappointed.

But as they proceeded the penny dropped that all the companies were once famous names which had failed, been taken over or faltered and recovered – names like IBM, Midland Bank, Sabena, C & A (the Dutch fashion house which withdrew from the UK), Pan Am, Apple. In pride of place was their own company as a name on a grave headstone!

It was shocking because at that point the bank was doing swimmingly well. Profits were still climbing and the share price still doing well too. 'Why fix what's not broken?', was a popular cry.

But the bank's executive leadership had decided that the time to fix it was before the sales-based model was a busted flush.

During the rest of the meeting, delegates were, for the first time, given the tools and the data to really get behind the apparently good numbers and to see the choice which the bank had to make between carrying on until the market turned against them or change the customer proposition preemptively, knowing that the transition was dangerous and short-term performance would suffer.

From there they attended mini vision workshops in which the future customer experience was sketched out. They could see that there was a future. And they had begun to grasp that the old model of banking needed to be replaced.

In the months that followed, the most persuasive change was the return to the bankers of some of the critical decisions which had been centralised. Branches were clustered into small local groups and encouraged to share experiences and practices and to take control of their local footprint.

As in the previous examples, management had realised that simply introducing a new strategy or approach without understanding the likely response of the implicated group would be likely to undermine the strategy. Alternatively by getting the implicated group involved in understanding their own likely reaction to a change gives that group a personal choice between actively participating and reverting to a trance-like state of a spectator – present but not engaged.

Seeing how others do it

In another example a media business was engaged in a major challenge to update its technology. A change which would alter irrevocably the jobs of many and the power balance between the shop floor and management. For months neither side would listen until an executive had the idea of some exchange visits with a competitor, which was way ahead on just such a change.

Seeing for themselves that to stand in the way would simply result in less business to negotiate over, the workforce agreed to participate in a change process which saw the arrival of new technology, new skills for those who wanted to stay and grow and good exit packages for those who didn't. The exchange visits had broken the log jam.

This story is similar to the much-told one about Southwest Airlines in the US where the ground crews were taken to see how race car pit stop crews had turned the stops into a tightly focused team experience performed at dizzying speeds. There was little lecturing at them, they could see the point right there in front of them.

It is worth remembering that many employees and managers who are institutionalised may simply not be able to see an alternative without physically seeing it in action and 'smelling the coffee'. Managers and consultants often don't understand that polished presentations are no substitute for seeing, touching and experiencing the alternative.

OTHER SIMPLE DEVICES TO HELP PEOPLE HAVE INSIGHT ABOUT THEIR PART IN CHANGE

The dinner party

A specialist team at a bank was attempting to undertake the transformation of its relationship and service proposition to its internal customers. It had organised a gathering of about 200 of the top specialists who would have to embrace and own the need and execution of the change. Many did not see the need for it or thought it was someone else's problem.

They arrived expecting the usual dreary line-up of PowerPoint presentations and were surprised to find themselves at eight in the morning sitting at round tables around a large dining-room table at which sat about eight more junior colleagues.

The lights dipped and the candles on the table flickered. The host at the dinner table was asking the group about the results of a recent poll about the progress of the transformation. The group was not slow to explore and debate the results and expose the reluctance of middle management – who comprised the wider audience – to embrace the change. The diners pulled few punches and the atmosphere in the room was mesmerising. Everyone was gripped by the spectacle.

Part way through the 'dinner', four empty chairs were filled by senior internal clients of the group. Attention turned to their perspective of the progress of the transformation in service offered to them.

In a half hour or so the whole group was engaged in a way that could never be achieved by the presentation of some survey results. Here was a group of staff risking their careers to tell it like it was. Mindful of the risks, the head of the function went out of his way to exemplify their behaviour as a role model for the transformation.

Of course this was no more than an attention grabber, but executives like the boss of this department increasingly know that they need to be the chief engagement officers as well as the specialists; they need to influence the drama of work.

Do-it-yourself culture diagnostic

It is sometimes the simplest things that create the energy to make people sit up and take notice. An engineering firm, outwardly worthy, wanted to make the re-energisation of their culture a differentiator in their employment market. At the outset they considered having an outside consulting firm conduct a survey of prevailing culture so that, in keeping with their engineering culture, they could organise a rational process of culture change.

They did no such thing, choosing instead to design their own. They asked for volunteers to record and role play the relationships between different departments. It was assembled as a series of cameo performances, with a connecting thread which was the impact that the internal culture had on clients. Having first entertained and shocked themselves they invited clients to see a reduced version and to discuss the changes they would like to see.

The exercise allowed the organisation to home in on key drivers of their culture which they addressed through some more traditional routes, safe in the knowledge that the diagnostic phase had caught the essence of what needed to be changed because it was conducted by those who would need to make the change.

Mystery shoppers

Most retail and service-based businesses use specialist outside suppliers to act as mystery shoppers. One organisation halved the scope of the external contract and enrolled staff to fulfil the other half, not knowing what the outcome would be.

Staff fell over themselves to join the scheme in which, as in community policing, there was a small extra financial reward, but the work had to be done in the employee's own time. The company found that whilst the outsiders were able to provide valuable benchmarking, their own people found new energy to beat the competition. Participants became standard bearers for service and the enemy was externalised.

And when it came to new customer service initiatives the organisation had a ready-formed group of volunteers.

The company fair

A major high street/shopping mall retailer was failing to cross-sell to customers not because their different product areas were being particularly political but because their service delivery staff were relatively ill-informed about the products and interplay across all the products and tended to stick to what they knew.

At a massive company fair every part of the business was invited to construct an accessible learning experience about their own product. The experience also included live theatre in which a whole variety of customer interactions were played out illustrating when and how the products should be associated and sold together.

Over a number of weeks every member of staff had a chance to visit and experience the fair.

LAST FEW WORDS

The diagnostic, whatever shape it takes, is the first part of engaging employees in the change. It can either be thought of as a clinical management tool which is done to people or it can be the first symbol of a different relationship between the change process and its sponsors.

On many, probably most occasions, organisations do not stop to make a choice between managing the diagnostics as a clinical top-down management exercise versus running it as an experience which will stimulate the insight of those implicated in the change.

Checklist
Predicting how previous approaches to engagement may dispose people to engage (as hooligans, collaborators, reformers).

Q   Among the sponsor team and internal advisers what experience and insight do we have about how previous approaches to engaging people may dispose them to react?

Q   As a sponsor team are we ourselves aware of how we have hitherto reacted to being engaged? What insights does this provide us about the disposition of the groups we are trying to engage?

Q   Do we rely on quantitative surveys which may be out of date and too general to help with the specifics of this change?

Q   Have we validated conclusions about how people may be disposed to respond to being engaged by bringing together groups representative of those to be engaged either physically or virtually by web-based diagnostic sessions? Do we participate in these to see for ourselves?

---

8 Preparing to Design an Effective Employee Engagement Intervention

This chapter is concerned with preparing a team to design an effective engagement intervention. By intervention I mean activities or experiences in which selected groups of employees or possibly every employee is invited to contribute to:

- solving a crisis;

- devising a business strategy or plan;

- creating a change or transformation programme;

- developing the brand/service experience.

The situation: you have come to realise that it is time to consider the involvement of employees beyond an inner circle in tackling the situation which the business finds itself in. You have formed a group which will think through the development of an engagement intervention both to help prepare the ground for change and, where it will add value, to involve groups of employees (or possibly everyone) in the formulation of the plan.

You have formed an engagement steering group comprising some of the organisation's leadership team and some from within the business. They are a new group and need to be prepped and equipped to come up with an approach. To do this you need to precede devising practical recommendations with a session or process called 'principles and lessons for designing employee engagement'.

PRINCIPLES AND LESSONS FOR DESIGNING AN ENGAGEMENT INTERVENTION

The thinking here, as elsewhere in this book, is not theoretical, it is drawn from the experience of consulting extensively in this area, specifically designing and executing practical mass employee engagement interventions.

Who should be involved in the design of the employee engagement process?

I favour a two-tier approach in which an inner core of the most radical thinkers push the envelope which is in turn tested with a much larger senate drawn widely from the implicated groups. The inner team, which should not be confined to the existing hierarchy, should be watchful for the inevitable forces of reactionary influence from 'old guards'.

The ideal design process has four parts. The foregoing is designed to summarise the thinking covered in earlier chapters as the basis for inducting the steering team:

1. what engages us?

2. understanding previous patterns of engagement of the engagement steering team;

3. considering which approach to engagement will add value to the business;

4. guiding principles which will result in creative employee engagement interventions.

1. What enagages us?

That the CEO or the sponsor of the change is the chief engagement officer is so obvious there should be no need for it to be stated. Yet in many if not most cases of change, the CEO or sponsor is often intimately involved during the front-end thinking but often disengages when it comes to planning the engagement of the broader population beyond the executive or elite design team.

Often by the time the strategy or change gets to the people who must execute it the engagement process designed to energise them has been reduced to a cascade in which the participants are turned into spectators. To avoid reverting to cascade solutions those designing engagement intervention should start by recalling what engages them at work.

Let me take you back briefly to the ice cream exercise in Chapter 2 in which I explored the characteristics used by people to describe the drivers which resulted in them being truly engaged in a work project or activity outside work such as a personal interest or charitable endeavour.

In hundreds of meetings in which I have asked people to record their most engaging project, people used these kinds of words and phrases to describe the drivers or conditions which helped to engage them:

• shocked to be invited to participate in such a key exercise;

- surprised at the level of creativity used by the company to set the stage for our involvement;

- trusted with something normally given to more experienced or senior people;

- stretched way beyond my normal comfort zone;

- into the unknown;

- made totally accountable;

- given the right amount of time, but not too much;

- saw the difference it made to the end result;

- blank piece of paper;

- an authentic invitation to influence decision making rather than a management exercise in 'making the staff feel involved' – a sentiment that employees feel patronised by and one which dumbs employees down.

These are the conditions in which people reported that they became really engaged. They talked about boundless energy, giving freely of their discretionary effort, taking great personal risks and unleashing their creativity; in short they took ownership. People take ownership and become 'committed reformers' when these conditions are present.

You may recall from chapter 2 that in recalling projects which really engaged them, some people went back many years and others had to recall past employers for the last time that they felt really engaged at work.

But all are united in the view that when engagement occurred that the key is being trusted to get on with work which adds value to the greater good.

Whenever I conduct these exercises I am struck by the change which comes over people when they recall the project that really engaged them: a fire in the eyes is ignited and a palpable sense of energy is created in the room.

My evidence suggests that real engagement is a common experience for those who have the power or discretion as to where to direct their energies, but a rarer phenomenon for those who are in the corporate machine where little leeway or discretion to influence decision making is provided.

Some leaders argue that command and control is the natural order. They say those with power have earned the right and have the responsibility to make most of the judgements and decisions affecting those whom they have responsibility for.

Our argument is simply that whilst that view represents the assumptions of the command-and-control era of leadership it deprives organisations of the wisdom, creativity and potential value which the people can add.

We therefore see employee engagement as a leadership capability which will add value to a change or every day in the line. But it involves more than the capability to involve the right people in decision making. It means leaders sharing power and reaching around the hierarchy to engage people. It involves becoming more guide than god. It involves being a great facilitator who can govern a more inclusive approach to decision making combined with the discipline to close down discussion and move on.

Opening up decision making – the core of employee engagement – and governing the process of engagement is exactly what is happening in mass employee engagement exercises.

The preamble to a newly formed engagement steering group should begin with the ice cream exercise in which participants can have their own insight about what being engaged means. By doing so they will conclude that creating an effective employee intervention means one in which people:

- have to discover facts and think for themselves;

- think through possible solutions and invent ways to compare and evaluate the risks and benefits of each of them;

- are thrilled to be responsible for execution because they see it as their own work.

In short the steering group must be in no doubt as to the difference between getting those implicated to do the work and 'making them feel a bit involved'.

Such a discussion ought to surface all the assumptions, fears and prejudices about employee engagement which need to be clarified before work can start.

2. Understanding previous patterns of engagement of the engagement steering team

I have no intention of repeating the last chapter which focused on involving large groups in developing their own insight about their place and disposition to act when engaged in change. Here I want to pause on the previous engagement patterns of the engagement steering group driving the process.

It is too easy for them to feel that they are not players themselves; that they are in some way above it and clinically disconnected. A degree of aloofness in change is no doubt a good thing. But the point here is that their role model to each other and to others is highly influential to colleagues observing them.

It's not about controlling every symbol and instinct that these people have. They will be ambitious people with big egos and it's impossible to choreograph them.

The route to creating an effective team role model lies in the personal insight which individual members of the team have about:

- the approaches to engagement which they have experienced as employees and which ones they believe they subconsciously or overtly admire;

- the influence that their own experience of being engaged in change has had on the approach to engaging others which they have adopted.

In my research into engagement, levels of self-awareness among leaders about their default approaches to engagement were very low. Most leaders that I have interviewed had never reflected on their own approaches to engaging others; to most it is an impulse, a reflex action shaped by their experience. In fact few leaders make a conscious choice between the approaches to engagement.

The insight that they have a choice of who to involve in the decision-making process must be accompanied by a willingness to review some of their assumptions about power. To manage engagement means that they will have to be willing:

- to share their power;

- to short-circuit old hierarchies;

- like a head chef they must be willing to lead the process of engagement by integrating the kitchen with the front of house.

Creating insight among teams about their own preferred and probably instinctive patterns of engagement is easily done by asking each team member to borrow from cognitive therapy by asking them to recall the last two change processes they have been instrumental in and to evaluate, from the shoes of an employee affected by the process, what approach to engagement they endured or enjoyed under their direction.

This should be accompanied by discussion about how their experiences, both as employee on the receiving end and as boss dishing it out, shapes their instincts about employee engagement. Clearly, having representatives from down and across the organisation will stop this becoming an ivory-tower conversation. By doing so the group will be prepared to consider the approaches to engagement which will add value to the current project; the next stage in the conversation.

3. Considering which approach to engagement will add value to the business

Let's remind ourselves about the four approaches to engagement in Figure 8.1.

Two of the biggest concerns expressed by CEOs about engagement are neatly summed up by these quotes:

- 'I'm worried that engaging broader groups will simply slow things down. Frankly my small exec group will get most decisions 80 per cent right most of the time and we simply don't have time to open it up to all and sundry.' Or as Martin Sorrel, boss of UK media group WPP famously said, 'I'd rather make ten flawed decisions on Monday and get on with it, than one good decision on Friday and miss the boat.'

- 'The last thing I want is to open up a can of worms with uncontrolled brainstorms all over the company which result in inconsistent practices or half baked ideas.'

In other words it is the trade-off between the promise, provided by engagement of a richer, perhaps more sustainable outcome, and the apparent speed of an executive decision taken without much, if any, consultation.

My challenge to CEOs and other leaders and supervisors who are concerned about the apparent slowness of engagement is twofold:

- *The limits of a one-trick pony.* If you are automatically selecting your default approach to engagement, either consciously or unconsciously,

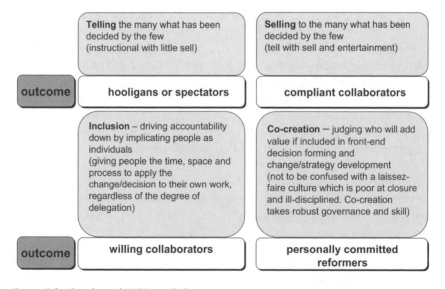

Source: John Smythe and McKinsey & Company

Figure 8.1   Four approaches to engaging people

you may be irrationally foregoing the benefits which other choices may offer.

As a team discuss the pros and cons of all four approaches and make a considered choice. If you have the discipline to go through the thinking with colleagues on this and future occasions a conscious team decision will be much easier to implement and explain to broader audiences beyond the steering team.

- *Dumbing down your employees.* If you have a distinct and repetitive pattern of engagement, your employees will become used to it. Should you decide to adopt a different approach to engagement on a future occasion they may well not be able to respond. They may have become stuck in a pattern of response. Thus the CEO who has had to clamp down or consolidate may get to the point where they want to open up the decision-making process to get the organisation on a growth path again. They want to encourage creative challenge but the populace, probably even their own exec, is wary of doing so. In this common situation the analogy of fitness is apt. Muscles which have not been used need stretching and practice. This CEO needs to explain what they have all been through and why there has been a period of tell and why now is good to open things up again. Care needs to be taken to avoid knee-jerk rejection of the first voices which challenge.

The challenge to leaders is to make the process of choosing an appropriate approach to engagement a core part of the change planning approach overcoming strong impulses to defer a topic which might usually be seen to be in the communication box, one which is left to the end of the traditional change and decision-making process.

Clearly if discussion of the approach to engagement is delayed until after the change programme approach is underway, a default – almost certainly a tell or sell – approach to engagement will automatically be selected.

Having made it an upfront decision the next challenge is to articulate the scope and boundaries of the invitation to make it clear to management, to those to be invited to participate and those to be excluded.

Constructing the invitation to engage the right people is a task for the sponsors of the change. The group needs to ask itself:

- What are the anticipated benefits of the chosen approach to engagement?

- What are the risks?

- Which groups or individuals will add value to the content or substance of the decision or change (and at what stages)?

- Which other groups may add value by advocating the proposed change if communicated with early but not actively engaged?

- Which specific aspects of the decision/change are the groups invited to contribute their ideas to?

- Will the engagement process be face to face or electronic and will some individuals be co-opted onto the change team?

- What process will be used to collect their ideas?

- What channel will be used to feed back how their ideas have impacted the programme?

Addressing these questions will enable the change team to put boundaries around the engagement and communicate clearly about it to those affected and directly implicated.

4. Guiding principles which will result in creative employee engagement interventions

This section deals with the ten principles of designing an engagement intervention and should be used to govern the design of the intervention.

The story which follows these principles embodies many of them. Without them it is highly likely that the engagement intervention will revert to traditional decide-and-tell cascades of varying degrees of novelty.

The ten principles are:

- shock, surprise and challenge;

- create a line of sight;

- self-discovery;

- experiential participation and suspending current realities;

- let the people do the work;

- remember the supervisors – manage the seniority effect;

- align the measures;

- equip the sponsors and the participants to engage;

- create widespread understanding of the scope of invitation and boundaries of the engagement;

- communicate how the engagement is impacting the decision or change.

Shock, surprise and challenge (avoiding the déjà vu effect)

On the face of it this is self-explanatory, however it is worth reiterating the metaphor about the chef. The chef must make sure that the novelty of the menu is complemented and supported by the front-of-house experience. They must manage the front of house as an integrated part of the experience.

Too often in change or day-to-day performance the novelty of the original thinking is undermined by the way that those directing the change or decision engage those who are key to execution. The danger is that the engagement and communication processes appear to be repetitions of past practices which dilute the novelty and freshness of the underlying strategy, change or decision.

The principle is that the engagement must shock, surprise and challenge people into taking notice. *CEOs and change sponsors should beware internal advisers peddling cautious reactionary approaches.*

However it is also worth noting that employees for the most part may require surprise but they do not want excess glitz or CEOs thinking they are celebrity performers. Most do not like the displays of CEO 'egotainment', which is so much a feature of over-staged puff-and-smoke events.

Create a line of sight (between the vision and its impact on the day-to-day job of those implicated)

In the research conducted with McKinsey and Company and Company into employee engagement I found that the front line showed different attitudes towards change, according to the type of engagement experienced. When invited to improve aspects of their own work in the context of a higher corporate objective, employees described themselves as being positive about it.

By contrast, if they were being invited to contribute to a programme which was felt to be corporate, distant or abstract (disconnected from their own influence), scepticism quickly spilled into cynicism, even when the intentions to engage were good and where their ideas were actually vital to capture. In the research we summarised these attitudes as follows:

People are particularly disengaged by:

- being marketed at and feeling like spectators;
- being promised one form of engagement only to hear the rules change midway;
- hearing too little about how their ideas are influencing the outcome.

People are engaged by:

- leadership demonstrating that they have considered who will add value;

- being clear about who will be engaged, in a way which sets the right expectations and lets everyone focus on their day job;

- setting engagement challenges in the context of their own work;

- experiencing role models.

'What does it mean for me?' is the question which must be answered. People are happy to have grand vision and plans laid out provided they can see and contribute to the bit which affects their day job, especially where they interact with customers. What they dislike are vacuous corporate programmes where the links with them are not made.

Self-discovery rather than corporate messaging about solutions

Leaders and employees are more likely to implicate themselves voluntarily and sustainably if the process of engagement has involved their active participation in discovering for themselves:

- the evidence for a case to change;

- where they fit in the case for change;

- solutions to the issue or change;

- the responsibility of weighing the pros and cons of solutions;

- their part in making it real.

Participants in a change often see the change only from the angle of the spectator. When they are required to become the teacher/facilitator about the change to others, they shift from spectator mode to being implicated members of the process. Giving employees a teaching role is a powerful way of giving them a stake.

Self-discovery is an important principle because most sheep-dip/cascade communication in traditional change communication casts people as spectators, where all or most of the answers are presented as 'ready to eat'. Self-discovery requires people to get off the employee couch and source the ingredients and cook it for themselves. Caught up in the process they become implicated.

I'd also like to take a moment to distinguish between those learning processes characterised by learning maps and real engagement interventions. The stated purpose of the learning map process is laudable. It is to help employees locate themselves in a change journey or service value chain so that they can understand better the part they have to play.

The essential truth is that these processes are designed to bring about compliance with a predetermined outcome. As a means to gain compliance and to extend understanding they are a useful tool. But they are not an authentic means of engagement because power is not being shared.

Experiential participation and suspending current realities

A sibling concept to self-discovery is making the engagement experience experiential. By experiential I mean participants being entered into an activity which surprises, shocks and challenges them to think freshly for themselves. Most organisations get no further than seating people in conferences or placing them in conventional learning situations, both of which tend to encourage a spectator response.

Equally important is to recognise that people are ensnared by the existing cultures. If you ask people to improve their existing performance they will waste a lot of time moaning about existing barriers to performance such as systems, bosses and so on. To encourage people to think out of their existing box we can suspend the existing organisation. I often do this by devising scenarios in which employees are cast into the role of predators or defenders where all or many current rules and assumptions are temporarily cancelled.

The travel industry case at the end of this chapter illustrates the idea of suspending existing realities.

Let the people do the work

An engagement intervention will be judged from the outset by the way it is organised. The design team ought to be well represented by the groups to be engaged. They will have the best sense of how to truly shock, surprise and challenge their own colleagues. Including them in up-front design also reduces the road-testing and pilot phase.

Remember the supervisors – manage the seniority effect

Look at most people development activity in big organisations and you will find that it is generally aimed at the top of the hierarchy. The same pattern exists for communication. There is a history of communication reflecting hierarchical conventions. Top people get more of everything. It is changing and technology is liberating information for the workers. But the seniority effect is endemic.

An exec or leadership group might be tied up for days with an engagement experience but by the time it reaches down it will probably be reduced to hours or have become compressed into a communication exercise; and thus be largely wasted.

American academic John Kotter, who has conducted research into employee attitudes during change, reports that employees take little heed of corporate messages during change. Their horizons are focused on the here and now and surviving the turbulence, except that is, when they are given the time and opportunity to discover for themselves their own place in the change process.

The point is not that everybody should be dealt with equally but that in planning the engagement groups which are critical to the change, they must be immersed to the degree necessary to implicate them in the process.

Communication alone will not cut through to them. CEOs and sponsors who short cut on the engagement process, believing that a cascade-type communication will get the message over, risk cutting the body off from the head. What looks like an efficient economy becomes useless noise in the organisation. In this situation employees feed back that the latest change is just another initiative about which they feel no ownership or responsibility towards.

Align the measures

A client of mine once remarked that his employee satisfaction scores among the thousands of retail staff reporting to him were still improving, despite the face-to-face feedback telling him the opposite when he walked the talk around the country. At the time he was putting through a radical change process which was affecting everyone's job. And he couldn't understand why the research was painting such an uncritical picture.

We reviewed the topics being canvassed in the routine employee satisfaction measure and drew the conclusion that they simply were not tapping opinion on the extraordinary change. They were focused on assessing satisfaction with some of the alleged drivers of employee satisfaction. And in subsequent conversations on the shop floor where staff were asked why the survey was not providing a balanced picture they responded by describing the survey as being irrelevant to the change process. They validated that they were pretty happy with pay, conditions, relationships with bosses and the like but could find no questions which enabled them to feed back opinion on the change.

So had my client not been sceptical and curious he might have thought that he had just spoken to a small minority on the shop floor. Shortly after, we devised a change poll designed specifically to measure:

- perceptions about the claimed business benefits of the change;

- perceptions about the experience of the change management process;

- views on the credibility of the engagement process being used to tap into employee knowledge and insight;

- role model examples of key sponsors of the change.

He had aligned his measures with the change in progress and learned that existing routine measures may be misleading and unhelpful.

Chapter six explores measurement in much more detail.

Equip the sponsors and the participants to engage

As in any soap opera the actors get used to their parts. The same is true in the workplace. Bosses get used to the performances which they repeat and employees become used to responding in predictable ways (see previous chapter). If a new boss arrives and decides that they want to engage the people in a change process, they will be well advised to understand the patterns of engagement adopted by leaders and followers during change. As I noted in the previous chapter, previous behaviour is the best predictor of future behaviour. If the boss wants to encourage new behaviours, the actors, both bosses and employees, will need rehearsals to give people the practice and the confidence to participate in the manner desired.

In practice this means that you cannot suddenly go from an autocratic top-down model to one in which you expect people to respond to a more inclusive approach. There will be distrust and a lack of collective skills. It will take experimentation. Readers should dip into Ricardo Semler's book entitled *Maverick* (2001, Random House Business Books); in it he tells the long journey he undertook to democratise decision making in his Brazilian company Semco.

Create widespread understanding of the scope of invitation and boundaries of the engagement

People need to understand what they have been invited to contribute to and be able to see the boundaries of the invitation. This is especially true if the invitation to contribute is a surprise, perhaps following a period of high control and compliance. People need to feel safe and be encouraged to engage. Sponsors of the process need to explain why the invitation is being extended, what value they believe the people will add and why it is worth the time and effort. Participants need to be reminded of the obligations of citizenship and how it will be governed.

Communicate how the engagement is impacting the decision or change

There is a critical role to be played by communication in creating widespread understanding about the engagement intervention and the business outcomes expected from it. Plus we know from our research in this field that continual communication about the process is key to its credibility. A global data company built a dedicated website to enable employees to track the impact of employee-generated ideas for the company's transformation.

These ten principles should help those setting out to design an employee engagement intervention to create something which releases value for the business and opportunity for employees.

To close this chapter on designing an effective employee engagement intervention I tell the story of a well-known company in the leisure sector. The story embodies most if not all the ten principles of designing an effective engagement intervention.

LEISURE COMPANY ENGAGES ITS ENTIRE STAFF IN DRIVING SERVICE AS A KEY DIFFERENTIATOR

In his early days the CEO of this company faced financial losses, poor staff morale and league tables across the sector which showed the whole industry how far this former icon had slipped. He focused on the fundamentals and over 3 years returned the company to within sight of the top of the field. Indeed in his fourth year the business achieved the highest margins in its sector.

He had restructured, driven costs down, developed new products and exploited every opportunity for advantage until only customer service remained as a source of competitive advantage. Even on service the company was already ahead of most of its traditional rivals on most criteria – but only just.

Holidays and travel is a sector where any innovation is aped pretty much overnight. Service, on the other hand, has the potential to put blue water between competitors. The CEO and his colleagues knew that a prescribed service by numbers approach would be inappropriate. It would have to be a service proposition which could be delivered voluntarily and willingly by staff.

Recent commercial success and high scores for service also meant that staff might have reacted by pointing to the research and saying: 'We're already ahead, what's the point of this exercise?' In fact they welcomed it with open arms because it was an initiative which gave them a greater role.

The plan was to engage everybody in the company over a 6-month period. Initially an engagement design group representative of the whole business was assembled. It had a bare 3 months to design the service initiative before 2000 of the company's top managers met in central Europe.

The service plan had two parts. The first consisted of a set of service improvements devised by the cross-company design group. These were essentially devised by quite senior management and were to be implemented across the group. They included:

- a customer loyalty scheme;

- a consistent, cross-business customer charter which expressed the quality of service customers can expect at any point of contact with the organisation;

- a 'service bible' for staff to use as a consistent business-wide reference to help guide their customer service activity;

- a 'customer service hero' award for staff providing outstanding customer service over specified periods of time;

- customer panels – periodic focus groups with customers to gain qualitative feedback on the reality of the service being provided;

- 'the small things that make the difference' – a range of locally determined enhancements aimed at differentiating the business at the point of customer contact.

But even these initiatives were extensively tested in business working groups which reached down to other levels of staff before finalisation. The six initiatives were to be put together and introduced to the business as the 'Secret Service Dossier' at the end of year gathering of 2000 managers. But there was a twist.

Creating a burning platform

The mass meeting of managers opened with upbeat reports and presentations in the usual vein. Then from the wings emerged a high court judge complete in his gown and wig. In sombre mood he advised the assembled group that whilst the benchmark research for customer research looked pretty good at first glance, anyone looking behind the data could see a situation in which the competition were closing the gap and that if he projected forward, under the assumption the rate of catch up would be constant, it would be a matter of a few months before the company was running neck and neck or even be surpassed by competitors.

He accused the group of complacency and called witnesses to the stand. Members of the executive committee were cross-examined and the judge interspersed these with home video clips which he and his team had taken in taped interviews with customers and companies admired for their service. These included Apple, Hilton, Honda, Vodafone, 02, Orange, HSBC and Lloyds TSB among others.

The judge concluded that not nearly enough was being done on customer service. He deferred sentence by giving the organisation until the same time the following year to show that it had what it took to pull ahead.

Suspending current realities

With that the judge was replaced by a figure who introduced himself as the operations director of a make-believe start-up company called 'Obsession'. He told a startled group that it was great news that they had all been headhunted by Obsession to start on a new genre of company built on great customer service and he introduced their new CEO who appeared by satellite TV to welcome them.

She began by reminding the group that the reason they had been poached from their old company was because it was the only one which the industry felt might make a leap in service, so it was obvious that she should focus her daring raids on staff on it.

The participants were transported into roles as members of Obsession. In another twist their new operations director reported that they had managed to secretly film a senior manager in their old company revealing the contents of the Secret Service Dossier to colleagues. He then advised the group that if they cared to check the contents of their folders they would find a copy.

As members of the new organisation, teams around the room were tasked with devising the best plans to implement the Dossier before their old company was able to do so; this was called the 'knock-out plan'.

Teams were next asked to put aside the Dossier and examine the total customer journey across the life cycle of a typical holiday (see Figure 8.2), and propose service improvements across the whole or in particular parts. In doing so they had to distinguish between proposals which cost nothing and had no contingent impacts between one part of the organisation and another, and those where there were contingent relationships and investment implications.

At the conclusion of the scenario, participants were asked to turn the best no-cost idea into action plans and submit the bigger ideas which had cost implications. To conclude the drama, a newsflash announced that Obsession had been so successful that the participants' old company had acquired it, so re-acquiring the staff.

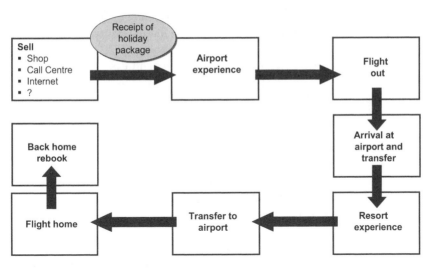

Figure 8.2   Total customer journey

Following the conference, the 2000 managers ran a similar engagement intervention across the entire company. Over the course of 4 months, all 12 000 employees participated in the same experience, learning about the customer service practices of other leading organisations, discovering for themselves that the only way to differentiate in their particular market was through sustained, exemplary customer service, and determining in their local work teams what they could do to make a difference to their own customers, internal as well as external.

So energised and focused has the business become on delivering exceptional customer service that it is now looking for ways to strengthen and sustain the customer service differentiation agenda. An 'Obsession Academy' is under development where all of the company's recruitment, induction and development will be brought together to ensure that customer orientation is the principal driver at the point of recruitment as well as the focus of development throughout the course of employees' careers. Modelled on the 'company university' programmes now well established in a growing number of organisations, the Obsession Academy will provide employees with self-development opportunities, self-managed and electronically delivered, supplemented with occasional 'real' learning activity.

The principle of self-implication can therefore be seen as the thread running through this entire programme: initially by the locally guided working parties coming up with the six early cross-business customer service improvement proposals; subsequently through the personal discovery experience provided by the Obsession total customer journey activity; and finally through the Obsession Academy where participation is not a requirement but where self-learning and personal improvement create powerful motivators for participation.

The experiment continues but this example exemplifies a bold intervention in a situation where there was no obvious or immediate burning platform. The CEO and his colleagues had judged that whilst the company was performing better than in the past few years it could be approaching another peak and that before it did so people should be given the opportunity to interpret market data and take action.

If you judge this engagement intervention against the four approaches diagram it contains a mixture of *sell* – the Secret Service Dossier is largely top-down – and *co-creational* in the second part of the scenario, where participants are invited to put aside the Dossier and make suggestions of their own. Not surprisingly the level of energy doubled – as it always does – when people are invited to co-create.

It is worth noting that the CEO in this case was no happy-clappy, power-to-the-people hippy. Far from it. Right from the start he kept emphasising that he hated brainstorms which were ungoverned, lacked closure and died 5 minutes after they finished. He was after no-cost, personally driven improvements that would encourage repeat purchase, build customer loyalty and reduce customer service costs – and that is exactly what he got.

I'll close this chapter on the design of engagement interventions with the four conditions which must be present for engagement to be successful and a checklist of some of the questions which a group designing the engagement should answer:

- The sponsors of change or strategy have overtly and rationally considered and decided, as part of the design of the change, who will add value to the project.

- The sponsors of change or strategy have designed and governed the process and experience of engagement so that it sets the right invitation to leaders and employees to participate in and contribute to the change, whilst developing themselves in the context of the change.

- Even when the discretion open to participants to contribute is small, the engagement experience should be characterised by learning through self-discovery, rather than by what seems like instructional communication.

- There must be value and benefit for both the organisation and its members.

Checklist

Designing and governing engagement as an integral part of strategy and change.

Q   Does the creative design of the engagement process look like it will deliver the chosen approach to engagement?

Q   Have representatives of the constituencies implicated in the change been involved in its design?

Q   Has a clear invitation which sets out the engagement contract been sent such that the process of engagement is understood by everyone?

Q   Has the principle of self-discovery for participants been followed in the design?

Q   Has sufficient thought been given to participants' skills? Will they feel able and safe to participate?

Q   Is the cost/appearance of the engagement in keeping with the project to hand?

Q   Is the communication process setting the right context for the engagement?

Q   Has the change head retained influence over the governance of the programme as it unfurls?

Q   Will the metrics measure the change to hand or will they measure a previous journey of change?

Q   Have those who need to make change contributed to measures of their own team's performance?

Source: John Smythe and McKinsey & Company

9 Brief Guide to the Methods and Approaches in Employee Engagement Interventions

This chapter builds on the principles of designing engagement interventions covered in Chapter 8. An engagement intervention is an experience in which the participants are invited to contribute their ideas. The experience can take a number of forms. Many of these have already been illustrated by the stories told earlier in the book. They include:

- creating a business game in which the current realities and barriers are suspended so that people can dream and think outside the box and then attempt to apply their ideas back into their own organisation (examples in this book include the travel/leisure company in which all global staff participated and the global medical company in which the top 180 people became the board to help create elements of a new business strategy);

- inviting people to solve problems or seize opportunities which would normally be tackled by higher levels of the hierarchy (examples in this book include the freight company in Chapter 1, the public utility which involved all implicated staff in achieving 40 per cent cost reductions and the global data company which enfranchised its entire staff in helping to turn the company around).

An intervention may be a temporary measure and may not result in permanent change to the leadership style and approach, although it may signal the desire to become more inclusive. The CEO of the utility company talks about engaging employees in decisions which affect them as a management or leadership philosophy.

It is fair to say that many leaders who want to create a more inclusive approach begin by experimenting with some sort of intervention in order to disarm critics who may say that a more inclusive approach is opening a can of worms which will be hard to close and will add little value anyway.

They probably share some of that anxiety and thus an intervention is a lower-risk experiment to begin the discussion. Ricardo Semler of Brazilian company

Semco experimented with including staff in key decisions over many years: it is not an overnight sinecure.

This chapter therefore provides further guidance on developing the kind of interventions illustrated by the travel and leisure example, the freight company and the global medical company.

I must first disappoint those expecting a painting-by-numbers approach to designing an employee engagement intervention. Employee engagement is an expression of a more inclusive approach to opening up day-to-day decisions and bigger-ticket change to those who will add value. It is not an off-the-shelf way to improve presentation of predecided decisions.

In the previous chapter I emphasise that the principles should be used to guide the bespoke design of an employee engagement intervention.

Here I cover:

- a review of some of the methods used in the stories we collected during the McKinsey and Company-sponsored research among 59 organisations and others from our consulting work in this area;

- some analysis of what kind of engagement interventions are suitable for the four approaches to engagement (telling, selling, inclusion, co-creation);

- a step-by-step guide to help those who are trying to build engagement capability into formal change programmes.

ENGAGING PEOPLE TO DRIVE PERFORMANCE IS A LEADERSHIP PHILOSOPHY NOT A TOOL BOX

One of the CEOs we interviewed for the McKinsey and Company-sponsored research into employee engagement describes employee engagement as a leadership philosophy, not a technique or channel. It is a part of the decision-forming process and as we have seen in Chapter 4 it tends to reflect a leader's instincts. It is often impulsive and repetitive in approach.

Thus those tempted to simply pick up the tools of an engagement intervention without attending to the leaders instincts and behaviours will probably be left with an intervention which cannot be sustained. To revisit the analogy of the chef used earlier, there is no point in redesigning the front-of-house experience if the food remains unchanged.

We have also argued in the last chapter that an effective employee engagement intervention must be designed to surprise, even shock and certainly to challenge. And therefore simply reaching for tried and tested traditional methods for cascading and campaigning to employees is futile. Treating employees as spectators is unlikely to start a process where people implicate and volunteer themselves.

GROUPING ENGAGEMENT METHODS UNDER THE FOUR APPROACHES TO ENGAGEMENT MODEL

In Figure 9.1 we have allocated some of the methods, tools and techniques used in employee engagement interventions, which I and my colleagues have designed or which were related to me in the course of the research for this book.

a *Telling* the many what has been decided by the few

- Low-key information campaigns drip-feeding news of apparently fragmented initiatives with little context, rationale or benefits
- Cascade briefings, executive road shows, profiles and interviews in internal newsletters, corporate videos
- Relies on instructional workplace activity for achieving compliance with associated targets and rewards
- Feedback/dialogue to check for compliance
- Change agents network that acts as a channel to deliver the message

b *Selling* to the many what has been decided by the few

- All the panoply of internal marketing communication and spectator-style events; use of entertainment
- Some attempts to collect ideas to influence change and/or to create a sense of involvement
- Scenario games in which people discover why decisions have been taken
- Opportunity for staff to explore evidence/data to develop the case for change themselves
- How we fit together experiences (e.g. route learning)
- Back-to-the-shop-floor symbolistic communication by bosses
- Employee suggestion schemes and staff attitude surveys that do not lead to change
- Direct input to staff from customers illustrating their experiences/issues
- Involvement in role play scenarios to understand behavioural and/or service standard challenges
- Change agents network that creates opportunities for people to participate in workshops to explore the rationale for change
- Celebration of achievement milestones

c *Inclusion*: driving accountability down by implicating people as individuals

On-the-job change in which participants:
- Undertake analytical tasks designed to create insight about the gap between their workplace performance or behaviour and skills and a desired end state
- Contribute to design metrics to self-evaluate their progress
- Re-fashion their own work within boundary set
Also
- Web-based consultation and learning
- Local task groups to work on solutions to problems
- Local task groups as part of a series of related and linked 'councils' across the organisation
- Developing clear definitions of expected behaviours, providing coaching to support individual change and metrics/measures to feedback and track personal progress
- Opportunity for staff to explore evidence/data to develop the case for change themselves and subsequently to propose options, solutions, metrics
- Involvement in role play scenarios to understand behavioural and/or service standard challenges with subsequent workshops to determine what to do
- Creating situations for people to learn about influencing skills by providing situations where they no longer enjoy their status-driven power base
- Corporate 'university' to equip people with the skills needed to take on board new responsibilities and expectations
- Change agents network that facilitates the development of experiences and opportunities for people to discover, learn and adapt
- Leadership development programme aligned with performance-management approach

d *Co-creation*: judging who will add value if included in decision making

- Business stimulation games in which challenges set are analogous to or rooted in real issues
- Giving people the actual business challenge/opportunity:
  - data gathering (conducting research)
  - hypothesis generation
  - solutions development
  - participation in decision making
  - design and executing engagement of others
- Shop-floor participation in designing engagement experiences
- Employee involvement which visibly influences the agenda
- Viewing the world from another's perspective: job swapping internally or experiencing different work settings outside the organisation designed to shift mindsets
- Specific issue workstreams led by people with specific responsibility and a clear brief and participated in by representatives from across the organisation
- Engagement workshops or local teams to identify a small number of high priority symbols/habits to change/develop

Source: John Smythe and McKinsey & Company

Figure 9.1   Methods, tools and techniques used in employee engagement interventions

Many of these techniques are referred to in the stories which pepper this book. But behind every story is an individual who takes a risk to engage their people in surprising and challenging ways. Whether it is the retailer which gives responsibilities back to branches, or the utility which implicates those who will be affected by decisions resulting in closures and job losses, or the boss of the leisure company who engages everyone in a drive on customer service, they are taking risks by engaging their employees in decisions traditionally taken by the few and imposed on the many.

Each of these leaders has designed and taken a very visible role in the method of engagement. They have not delegated the engagement completely to others.

Keeping the sponsors of change or the decision makers involved in the design and execution of the engagement process is key to success. A good way to start is to build engagement into the change model. The process described in the next section is presented as a half-day, step-by-step format, which any change team should be able to follow, especially if the facilitator is familiar with some of the ideas from earlier parts of the book.

BUILDING ENGAGEMENT INTO CHANGE PROGRAMMES

The process described here originates from consulting with a large number of clients. All had one requirement – to build the people dimension into change.

Specifically they wanted to be able to:

- factor people considerations into project management;

- flag risks arising from people issues before they became problems;

- flag opportunities to improve the project by involving the right people in the decision-forming stage and subsequent implementation;

- allow time for design of experiential activity, for production of communication materials and the organisation of logistics.

Many clients were motivated to think about more inclusive approaches to employee engagement by seeing and experiencing how programmatic change processes had alienated the people and often become unstuck during implementation.

Employees report that change programmes result in the apparent suspension of values and relationships. The programme office approach is said to legitimise temporary behaviours which are at odds with the 'way things are done around here'. This is hardly surprising as very often that's the exact intent. There's nothing wrong with speed and decisiveness; but all too often it is accompanied by a top-down approach to decision making and ideas generation.

Take the case of the European manufacturer where elite teams corrected quality problems on the manufacturing line and over the short-term observed improvements in the delivery of manufactured product. But in the medium-term, because the line workers had been shut out of the remedial process, they had lost their confidence to re-assert their voice and as a result quality problems re-emerged largely because the short-term fix was over-reliant on more senior management and consultants.

In retrospect, management wished that they had enfranchised the front-line staff into the remedial process both to add their ideas and to create sustainable ownership by them.

The engagement model which follows is based on a half-day exercise in which members of a change team work through a process designed to prompt discussion about employee engagement covering the following topics:

- agreeing what the concept means to them and what value might be added from integrating engagement into their change process;

- identifying which audiences will be implicated by the change;

- identifying which audiences may add value if involved early before the scope of change is agreed and which audiences may add value if involved in the design of execution;

- the methods of engagement which may be suitable;

- implications of engaging people on the overall project schedule – unless employee engagement is considered up front the train will have left the station and employee engagement will become employee communication after decisions have been taken.

This half-day session is designed to help a change team to pause and consider approaches to employee engagement whilst there is still time to integrate it into the overall project schedule and philosophy. Let's remind ourselves that the employee engagement agenda is not nice to do for the sake of the employees. It is a must-do if we want to add the value which some of the employees can bring to the design of the project in hand.

It is also a must-do if the organisation has attempted top-down imposed change and seen it fail or half succeed because the employees are barely cooperative. This was the case in the freight company in Chapter 1. If the new CEO had attempted to impose his will he would have failed like his three predecessors. He knew that he had to change the nature of the relationship between staff and management before he could attempt any reform of work processes; and he knew he could only do that if he brought them into management's tent and shared some of the decision making with them.

Of course a half day does no more than get the question of employee engagement onto the change agenda. But it will provoke the big questions to be posed: what is employee engagement; do we think that communication after the fact is employee engagement; what are the risks of not engaging the right people early on; what do we have to build into the overall project plan to make it happen?

The exercise has six steps or questions:

- Step 1 – What does engagement mean to me? What value might be added?

- Step 2 – Mapping the audiences: are our relationships with key groups healthy enough to let us succeed?

- Step 3 – What engagement approach will add value?

- Step 4 – Scope and boundaries: what is the invitation to groups we want to engage?

- Step 5 – What type of intervention will work?

- Step 6 – What are the implications of employee engagement on the overall project schedule?

Figure 9.2 is used during the six steps. It is a way of representing what can sound like a 'soft' discussion as a process which needs to be managed as part of the overall project plan.

The ideal participants in the discussion are the core change team or management team and, in keeping with the spirit of this book, a representative group of those affected by the change. One of the tenets of employee engagement is to give the work to the people.

Step 1 – What does engagement mean to me? What value might be added?

Source: Istockphoto/ Todd Harrison

The first step involves asking people what engagement means to them. Conduct the ice cream exercise in which the group is asked to work briefly in pairs to tell each other a story about a change project at work which really engaged them and which added value to the enterprise. Specifically ask the group to identify the conditions or drivers which brought about their engagement.

It need only take a half hour but it will take people out of their day-to-day preoccupation and put them in touch with what engages them, so they will have some personal insight about what engages others and more importantly, what disengages others during change.

Audience	Approach to involvement		Primary outcomes	Methods of engagement	Timescales	Responsibility /single sign-off	Production logistics/ implications
1.	a	b		-			
2.				-			
3.				-			
4.	c	d		-			
5.				-			

Figure 9.2   Engagement process

Most people will report that it involves being trusted with a project or responsibility which they have high discretion over and clarity of scope. They will recall being very animated by lofty challenges which were important to the organisation and they will remember working in unusual groupings. None will report being engaged by a cascade which tells them what has been decided by others!

An additional exercise is to ask the group – again in pairs at first – to reflect on the last change they sponsored or experienced and to:

- recall the pattern of engagement on that occasion;

- describe that pattern and which groups if any were engaged in the process;

- describe the outcome;

- decide if they would do it differently if they were starting again.

These two discussions will get the group into the topic and beyond a possible working assumption that communication equals engagement.

From this initial personal discussion about what engages individuals the group needs to ask itself what value will be derived from integrating engagement into their change process, perhaps using the prompt in Figure 9.3.

Step 2 – Mapping the audiences: are our relationships with key groups healthy enough to let us succeed?

Before getting practical I like to ask these groups what is the health of the relationship between the organisation (and with this team) and the groups affected by the programme. A simple question will suffice such as, is the relationship:

- red

- amber or

- green?

Q. What value will be derived from integrating our engagement into our change process for:

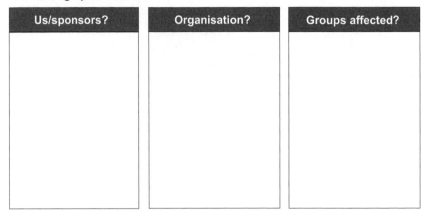

Us/sponsors?	Organisation?	Groups affected?

Figure 9.3   Value of engagement

And why is it like this? Some of the answers will have been provided in Step 1 in response to the reflections about engagement patterns in past change. I would direct you back to Chapter 7 in which I look at the imprisoning affects of past patterns of engagement at work and at home.

The point to make is that unless we consciously decide what approach to employee engagement will add value we will probably repeat past patterns without thinking about it. And as we know surprise is a key element of engaging people.

That done it will be useful to undertake a simple analysis of the demographics so that we are reminded of who we will be dealing with:

Q.   Which groups/individuals may have something to contribute to initial project scope?

–

–

Q.   Which groups may have something to contribute to project design?

–

–

Q.   Which groups may have something to contribute to execution or implementation?

–

–

Q.   Which groups will be sympathetic or potentially supportive?

–

–

Q.   Which groups/individuals may not be sympathetic and why?

–

–

Q.   Which other projects may this one most complement?

–

–

Q.   Which other projects may this one conflict with?

–

–

Step 3 – What engagement approach will add value?

The group should then use Figure 9.4 to list key audiences and debate which approach to engagement will add value for each and determine if an overall approach to engagement will be applicable.

It is here that heat should be generated around whether we have enough time and the value that employees may provide. The discussion should not lead people to the view that *co-creation* is the only game in town. It is to have a considered debate about which approach will add value.

Audience: what approaches to involvement will add value?

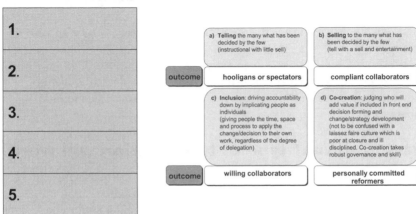

Source: John Smythe and McKinsey & Company

Figure 9.4   Audiences: approaches to add value

This is the moment to remind people what they said when asked early on about what engages them as individuals. It won't be an implementation schedule from the programme office.

To take the emotion out of discussions about whether there is time for engagement I find that it is worth weighing the risks and rewards of each of the four approaches for each of the key audiences. What you will end up with is a mix. And it is surprising how many old hard-line command and controllers will respond well to a discussion about risks and rewards. It turns a soft subject into a hard one.

This discussion will spill over into the next question – scope and boundaries: what is the invitation to groups we want to engage? This is an essential question because it goes most of the way to answer those who are still worrying about opening the proverbial can of worms.

Step 4 – Scope and boundaries: what is the invitation to groups we want to engage?

Having discussed the approached to engagement in Step 3 the change team should reflect on the specific added value they would like to invite different groups to contribute. This should also include the boundary of the invitation. What does this mean? In the case of the utility company which had to cut costs by 40 per cent, the invitation to staff to propose how this might be achieved by balancing the interests of staff, customers and the business, the target of 40 per cent was not negotiable. The firm of lawyers which wanted to involve its associates in more decisions put boundaries around the day-to-day decisions which affected their work.

The travel company which engaged its entire staff in developing a customer service strategy made it clear that ideas which would require budget or involve other parts of the business would be subject to agreement.

Agreeing boundaries means that expectations can more easily be set with the organisation.

The section of the schematic shown in Figure 9.5 can be used to identify desirable outcomes and boundaries for the design and implementation phases:

Step 5 – What type of intervention will work?

Earlier in this chapter I provided a list of some of the methods which are available to engage people. At this juncture, it must be said that all the principles of designing an engagement covered in Chapter 8, must be squarely introduced into the discussion as a test of the design.

Primary outcomes

Audience	Design	Implementation
1.		
2.		
3.		
4.		
5.		

Figure 9.5   Desirable outcomes and boundaries

Those principles are:

- shock, surprise and challenge (avoiding the déjà vu effect);

- create a line of sight (between the business outcome – the vision expected from the change, the overall change process or decision, its impact on the day-to-day job of those implicated and the role of every person affected by the change/decision);

- self-discovery;

- experiential participation/suspending current realities;

- let the people do the work;

- remember the supervisors – manage the seniority effect;

- align the measures;

- equip the sponsors and the participants to engage;

- create widespread understanding of the scope of invitation and boundaries of the engagement; processes of governance;

- communicate how the engagement is impacting the decision or change.

This is the point where the group needs to decide between the two principal types of possible engagement intervention:

- creating a business game in which the current realities and barriers are suspended so that people can dream and think outside the box and then attempt to apply their ideas back into their own organisation;

- inviting people to solve problems or seize opportunities which would normally be tackled by higher levels of the hierarchy.

Consideration should also be given to whether the engagement intervention is delivered as part of existing face-to-face meeting schedules, at the place of work or online; as intranet functionality progresses, online or through the desktop will be a routine part of engaging in change.

The book has many examples of how others have approached the creative challenge. Each challenge is different and the form of the intervention will be a function of the creativity of those present and the degree of risk that the sponsors have appetite for.

But by this stage in the session the group will have become a creative team and the ideas will flow. In the next chapter I tell the story of staff from a finance function who designed an engagement intervention for 150 people involved in a change process. They started unsurely but finished with 2 days of activity which would have blown the socks off any specialist creative team. It included writing the software for panel games they ran and creating sophisticated choreography of 150 people. Any group at any level can, with the right brief and a little professional guidance, design the engagement intervention. And something designed for the people by the people will be owned by the population to be affected unlike externally created solutions or ones created by some worthy elite.

Figure 9.6 can be used to capture the first thoughts. It is at this stage that the presence of those to be affected will add tremendous creative ideas that will work for their groups.

Aside from thinking about the methods, the team needs to think through timescales both for the design phase of the engagement and the execution. Too often change teams work under the assumption that once they have contributed to the creative design of the engagement process it will appear

Preferred methods and timescales

Audience	Design	Execution
1.		
2.		
3.		
4.		
5.		

Figure 9.6   Methods and timescales

overnight. By planning it properly, it is more likely the engagement that is experienced on the ground will resemble the intentions of the originating team.

Distinguishing between design and execution is also important to get the whole group to think through sequencing for different groups.

For instance in designing the engagement for the leisure sector company featured in the last chapter, it only became clear that there had to be an amended engagement experience for different groups once the senior management team had thought the implications of having a common approach through. Having done so, it was realised that there needed to be an assessment phase for bottom-up ideas arising from the shop floor so that choices could be made about which ideas to invest in and support and which ones to politely decline.

Had the senior group only taken an interest in the initial phases of the engagement process – for the more senior levels – there would have been confusion and false expectations set among the wider group of staff below the top 2000 or so managers.

This extract from that story also illustrates the seniority effect referred to in the principles section in the last chapter. The seniority effect, as the label implies, describes how engagement can often be a rich and deep experience for senior managers and a shallow and narrow one for those below.

Step 6 – What are the implications of employee engagement on the overall project schedule?

As we are talking about a conversation with a change team it is a good idea to tie everyone in to a governance process for the engagement and agreement on responsibility for the production and logistical aspects of the intervention (see Figure 9.7). In this way the engagement becomes a part of the change rather than an adjunct.

By completing the production/logistical implications box, the team will be required to think through the practical implications of their programme and the time needed to see it through. Too often this is delegated and poorly executed.

Finally the change team should be signing up to an engagement measurement process enabling them to assess the following (see the last part of Chapter 6):

- understanding of the business case for the change;
- understanding of the vision of how things will improve;

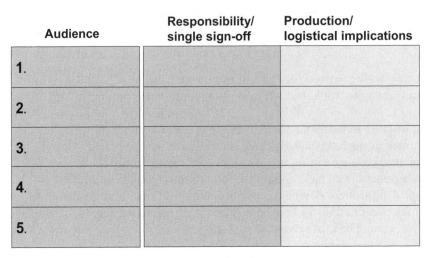

Audience	Responsibility/ single sign-off	Production/ logistical implications
1.		
2.		
3.		
4.		
5.		

Figure 9.7   Responsibility and production

- understanding of the overall timing;

- visibility and connectedness of streams/projects;

- degree to which people feel personally implicated;

- visibility of engagement activity;

- accessibility of the engagement activity;

- perceptions that people have about the invitation to contribute, challenge and feedback.

Having navigated through this agenda you will have a group which has thought through the employee engagement agenda and developed at least the basis for an intervention which will capture the insights and values of those affected.

10 Engagement to Drive Implementation of Strategy

In the previous two chapters I focused on the design of engagement interventions which will form part of a much larger approach to transforming an organisation. The core message to readers in these chapters was to consider who will add value to the change at the front end of the change process, before the change train leaves the station and builds momentum.

I am trying to break the convention that the people dimension is the last consideration, which reinforces the assumption that an elite few know better than the many.

In this chapter I hope to illustrate that the principles and tools of employee engagement discussed in Chapters 8 and 9 are also relevant to those driving the implementation of business strategy. To illustrate this, I have chosen the transformation of the finance function comprising close to 4000 people in a global financial services brand.

A FEW WORDS ON STRATEGY

Michael Porter described strategy as 'the creation of a unique and valuable position, involving a different set of activities'.

Henry Mintzberg draws out the distinction between deliberate and emergent strategy, pointing out that most strategy is a mixture of the two. Few can claim that they implemented a precise plan without making alterations as the situation changed on the journey.

Many business executives today would admit that things change so fast and so much that they have all but given up the pretence of creating strategy. They say that for the most part they react to events, bearing out Mintzberg's view that much strategy is emergent.

To paraphrase Ronald Heifetz of the John F. Kennedy School of Government, Harvard University, the difference between a manager and a leader is partly defined by whether they remain on the dance floor of day-to-day business, reacting and coping to immediate and present pressures, or ascend onto the balcony to seek out the next hilltop to aim for.

THE TRANSFORMATION OF THE FINANCE FUNCTION STORY

In this chapter I tell aspects of the story of the transformation of a critical functional department – finance – in a large and global corporation. The strategy word is usually invoked in the context of a whole organisation. In this case, the host organisation had come close to catastrophe under the previous administration, which had been led by a man with global ambitions for the organisation. He had expanded the organisation on the world stage but had gone many steps too far. The rescue squad set in place a crisis recovery plan which first focused on the bare essentials of good housekeeping, before embarking on the transformation of the brand.

The initial turnaround of the corporation took the best part of 2 years and it was in the early stages that the character at the centre of this story became the finance director. He had previously turned around one of the regional business units in the same organisation following an acquisition and a long-put-off integration of the merged entity. It had gone on to become one of the most profitable parts of the whole corporation.

His new task, the transformation of the finance function, was Herculean.

The story illustrates the balance to be struck between remaining on Heifetz's dance floor and ascending onto the balcony to set a direction. It also illustrates how employee engagement played a vital part in the transformation of the department by giving prescribed discretion to the people to implicate themselves in the transformation.

The strategy, simply stated, lay in creating a unique, valuable and above all reliable internal finance service so that the transformation of the organisation could be reliably tracked.

The start point was inauspicious. The finance function was slow in delivering accurate and timely data to top management which had prevented them from tracking the impact of radical change. Financial reporting was haphazard and external critics excoriated top management for this.

In short, the corporation could not be turned around unless the finance function was in the vanguard of the organisation's recovery. The state of the department owed much to the rampant expansion of previous years. Country organisations had developed their own functional capability and fostered a lack of transparency on their financial performance, little focus on cash flow and a disregard for the impact of their decisions on the company's balance sheet.

For 18 months the focus had to be on radically improving the basic function of providing accurate and timely financial data. Without this essential radar-screen, management were partially blind. Many improvement projects were initiated and very significant progress was made. The situation was so challenging that the incoming finance director and his team did not want to make any early claims of success.

They were so mired on the dance floor getting the finance team to dance to basic steps that little good news about progress made its way onto the street. Staff could be forgiven for thinking that not much progress was being made at all. Morale was not good.

Cast your mind back to the beginning of Chapter 2 where I invited you to transport yourself into the shoes of a mid-level employee experiencing a change process. In this case, over the first 18–24 months, the mid-level employees had witnessed the implementation of a variety of tighter disciplines but had no sense that these were part of an overall plan to transform the function; it was just more stuff to do.

How a key implementation activity sparked the need for a wide-ranging-vision engagement process

The insight to use employee engagement techniques to help drive the strategy occurred as a result of the debut of a shared-services project which involved the off-shoring of a significant part of the basic manual work of the function.

The off-shoring project was just one of the many streamlining projects which were part of the overall scheme to improve the performance of finance.

But this one would be very visible and would lead to at least 500 jobs being exported to a lower-cost location and in Europe that meant adhering to European legislation on workplace consultation, which varies from country to country. It would also mean creating an engagement process which would engender trust through honesty.

A country-by-country negotiation process was set up with local management where the rationale for the programme was discussed and the consultation process designed for each. Unusually, the centre went to the countries and it was described by them as an exemplary way of engaging them in the implementation of the shared-services (off-shoring) strategy.

Throughout the engagement of the country management teams, the centre team found itself constantly having to explain the vision or strategy for the whole of finance and how this shared-services initiative fitted into a bigger picture. It sparked a realisation that everyone ought to have the whole story about the strategy for finance so that they could see how all the implementation activities going on across the whole of the department fitted together.

It coincided too with a certain rising of confidence levels among the finance team's top management as improving the basics took effect.

The insight that it was time to wrap all the changes up as one story occurred because of the need to explain that off-shoring was not itself the strategy, it was one part of a much wider plan which had never been shared.

Ascending to the balcony

The executive team met and reviewed their progress and developed the rationale for articulating and engaging everyone in the vision for the finance function.

Looking back, the team decided that engaging all 4000 or so people in the vision for finance would:

- make visible to everyone the work that had already been undertaken to transform the finance function by making the connections between all the back-to-basics projects.

Looking forward they decided it would:

- help everyone in finance focus their time and creativity on:

  - executing existing initiatives and processes which would clearly help transform finance;

  - dropping or delaying work which was a distraction to fulfilling the strategy;

  - identifying new initiatives and processes which would help in very specific ways to accelerate the strategy;

- create a story shared by everyone about the transformation of finance which made clear the connections between all its elements.

Transferring ownership for local execution

A series of engagement sessions was planned in every country, the purpose of which was to achieve the ambitions described above in the vision for finance. The executive group were rightly wary of undertaking a communication cascade which would simply result in raising levels of awareness about the vision. What they primarily wanted to do was to build momentum behind local execution of the vision.

By local execution they meant generating insight in local teams about their own role in bringing about the vision.

In the engagement sessions, members of the exec attempted to strike a balance between setting direction and calling for local ideas to drive ownership and impact.

And as in any groups used to listening to the answers from bosses, most of the meetings started with a wall of faces silently shouting: 'What do we need this for?'

Many of the meetings were large, a hundred plus. But interaction was guaranteed using some simple and easy-to-facilitate methods which I will try to explain. To do so I need to provide readers with the basic story which was conveyed to the participants.

The train leaving the tunnel analogy

Source: Getty Images

It was important that the executives leading the engagement sessions started the sessions by acknowledging that the executive team had the advantages of the engine driver of a train leaving a tunnel. They had the best view and could see some of what was coming ahead, whilst most employees were still in the tunnel and could only see each other and today's work. But employees knew that the train was rushing to a new destination and that those at the front of the train were taking them there, but that they were saying little about why or where.

Executive team members also needed to acknowledge what the employees intuitively knew: that they had not been confident enough or motivated enough to relay the picture from the front of the train to the metaphorical screens in each of the carriages until now.

In other words, the senior executives had to give some of the psychological context before ploughing into the vision.

To return to the image of the train leaving the tunnel, people need to understand and be connected with the journey which they find themselves being taken on. Being taken anywhere in the dark at high speed by people who are reluctant to reveal their hands is, to say the least, unsettling. And that is, by and large, the experience of change most people report. Employees also often assume that they haven't been enfranchised as a deliberate keep-them-in-the-dark plan.

The sad truth is that most leadership teams do not keep people in the dark deliberately. Some do not see the need for it, but most want to wait until things are looking better and they feel more confident. But the later they leave it, the harder they have to work to instil confidence in their people; an invisible plan inspires no one.

Most employees would rather know the reasons for an overall strategy and the underlying substance as decisions are made, especially if they are not being invited to contribute to the decisions. And most will accept a top-down, tell approach if it can be explained why a tell approach is the best route on this occasion.

In this case the executives disclosed, each in their own way, some of the psychological context for the meetings, before sharing the initial articulation of the vision for finance. They did so to get reaction to the direction of the vision and more importantly to set the ground for turning some of the ownership for implementing the vision over to employees. What they were after was local action more than appreciation.

The diagrams which follow represent the core ideas that were discussed with participants. Figure 10.1 is the vision at a glance: it attempts to describe the 'from – to' which the function was attempting under four headings:

- our aspiration
- our expertise
- our transformation
- our people.

Figures 10.2 to 10.4 provide further detail.

To us as onlookers, the words may not seem to do justice to the underlying requirement to transform the finance function into a credible intelligence service. But to the workforce of the function, the words signalled a revolution. It's perhaps also worth noting that there will always be a silent or noisy stand-off by those preferring to frame the change as incremental and those who want it to be revolutionary.

In this case the critical challenge was to transfer ownership and energy to the whole 4000 employees. The finance director was determined to frame this strategy as revolutionary in the sense that it had to be done quickly and done by everyone, not just a handful of elite executives. The whole community of employees needed to embrace it.

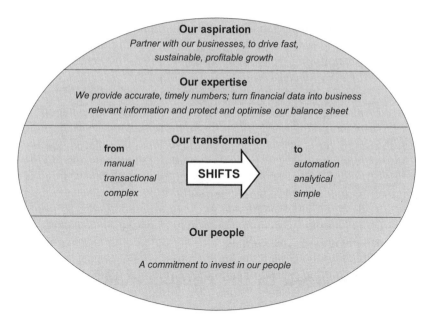

Figure 10.1   Finance – vision at a glance

Our aspiration

> *Partner with our businesses, to drive fast, sustainable, profitable growth*

- We aim to create a world beating finance function that helps to set the agenda internally, is a valued partner in the development of platforms for exploiting opportunity across our businesses and is recognised as a leader in accelerating the pace of change for profitable growth.

Figure 10.2   Our aspiration

Our expertise

> *We provide accurate, timely numbers; turn financial data into business-relevant information; and protect and optimise our balance sheet*

- We intend that business colleagues seek and respect our view as we work with them to inform and guide decisions. We will achieve this through detailed and timely financial analysis based on mastery of accurate data.

- We will offer judgement and insight on prevailing business issues, performance trends and opportunity as a result of a detailed understanding of the numbers.

- We will strengthen and protect the Group through our expert balance sheet management.

- We will maintain our lead through the recruitment and development of the best finance people in the industry.

Figure 10.3   Our expertise

Our transformation

Transactional to analytical	Manual to automation	Complex to simple
• We are shifting to a role that provides exceptional value and leadership to the company. • Our emphasis will be on analysing and using our information for business advantage and higher profit.	• We aim to streamline and automate much that is currently done manually. This will free up resources to focus on analysis and insight and enable us to build speed, greater accuracy and improved flexibility in all that we do.	• Complexity kills our ability to be fast, focused and effective. We are driving for simplicity through common approaches, centralised processes and effective support systems.

Figure 10.4   Our transformation

Giving the work to the people; making it personal

In the engagement sessions after the introduction and psychological disclosures referred to above, delegates were asked to focus on the three shifts in Figure 10.4. To get around the sense of being one in a crowd of a hundred, people were asked to work in trios or pairs to identify all the projects and initiatives that they had knowledge of which they believed had already started to address each of the shifts.

Given that they had all been involved in many apparently separate initiatives, they were able to populate large matrix charts with the projects which they had identified.

Letting people see that they have already been closely involved in working towards addressing the three shifts enabled people to feel that they already had ownership. And working in small groups, especially in this multi-language environment, generated terrific energy.

It meant that the facilitators could move the groups quickly on to address the real agenda of accelerating local execution of the three shifts and identifying where there might be opportunities for inter-country collaboration. Still working in their small groups they were tasked with promoting ways which they could take a personal role in making it happen in their own teams and promoting cross-country ideas which the regional head could syndicate.

Finding the balance between country ownership and top-down control

These sessions, under the leadership of the country heads, rippled out across the whole of finance, spurred on and governed by two control mechanisms. The first was a series of vision polls which tracked understanding of the vision, opportunities provided by country management to get productively involved and the visibility of management in championing the engagement process.

The second control process was the prospect of a forthcoming meeting of the whole executive at which each member was asked to provide a summary report of the impact of their local engagement process.

The two control mechanisms meant that the engagement process was left to the country heads but that the delegation was balanced by the accountability stimulated by the controls.

By the time of the executive meeting the leaders of finance had created some of the energy necessary to drive the vision down to bring about local execution, using the engagement programme.

Readers may recall the message from Chapter 4 'The irrationality of leaders in engaging their people in strategy and change' that most leaders make instinctive choices about the approach to engaging their people. Our choices tend to reflect the experiences we ourselves have been subject to and our comfort zones. In this case the leader much preferred to encourage his senior colleagues to draw their own conclusions about taking the initiative of engaging their own people rather than attempting to manage in an instructional style.

His is a *co-creational* style balanced with the strong controls referred to above. His choice of approach to engagement is based on the insight that his own executive team are more likely to employ a co-creational approach with their own people if they have experienced the same approach from him. His rationale is that if his own group take ownership of the vision process they will implicate themselves in the process and, in turn, if they offer their own people a co-creational approach, bounded with clear controls, they too will implicate themselves and make change happen at their own level. As a result there will be voluntary action to execute the three key shifts described earlier which are the key to transforming the finance function.

In this way the leader of the finance function intended to bring about a velvet revolution without the necessity for a traditional *tell*, command-and-control style change process.

A typical hallmark of the command-and-control style of change is the thirst by senior executives for getting the message out. A top-down change relies on copious corporate communication to make the change feel inevitable. But it cannot replace the real ownership which derives from well-judged engagement.

Is there a difference between command and control and well-governed co-creation?

Readers would be right to harbour scepticism. Is the head of finance simply not exerting his will by cleverly manipulating his people into thinking that they have more discretion than they really have over a prescribed agenda?

Let's look again at the facts. The finance function needed a new strategy. Few or none of the citizens of finance would argue otherwise. The executive team readily saw the case for change and were party to the design of a new vision. They participated in the articulation of the vision cited above. And in fact the engagement process which started with the generation and articulation of the vision and extended to the grass roots was patchy; it relied on the executive team volunteering to run it in their domains in a co-creational fashion, which more or less mirrored their own experience.

As a witness to much of the process, I observed some of the executives taking the risk to engage their subordinates by involving them in the decision-making process and seeing the creative energy and ownership which was triggered. I saw executives, more used to deciding and telling and being seen to be in control, being willing to say: 'I know some of the things we need to do to transform ourselves, but you will know more and different things to me.' They were willing to share power, albeit within the framework of the vision process.

I think you could argue that it was clever manipulation or that it was a genuine opening up of decision making and execution. Followers of French philosopher Foucault will hear echoes of his contention that engagement is simply part of the capitalist plot to enslave the workers in ever more devious ways!

His concerns should keep us alert to the truly cynical leaders who will use any means to raise productivity and returns. In that sense his Marxist perspective is a useful check on just that sort of exploitation of the concept of engagement. Engagement is already spoken of by some pundits as just another tool to drive productivity or retain people without the essential insight that a sharing of power is a prerequisite to real engagement. Recalling the words of the CEO of a utility company: 'Employee engagement is a leadership philosophy first, a management process second.'

Workers respond well to authentic engagement. They will volunteer and give their creativity if it is honestly sought and if value is added by their labours; and they will enjoy their work more and be inclined to stay and repeat the experience.

On the other hand, the workers also have nostrils as powerful as any gun dog's when it comes to sniffing out inauthentic motivations. They may not be able to specify exactly the nature of the deceit but they will know that something is not quite right. A dictator masked in the wardrobe of engagement will soon reveal his real beliefs.

It is worth reminding ourselves of the truths, both kind and cruel, which are told by the organisation's satirists and humorists who reside in every team. Whether their thoughts are recorded on blogs, at the water cooler or fed back to management, they will soon express and editorialise the zeitgeist more accurately than any company propaganda.

The merger of Guinness and GrandMet created the now global drinks firm Diageo. The new name was just 20 minutes old before an email did the rounds: Don't Imagine Any Great Employment Opportunities!

Framing and communicating the process

In Chapter 8 'Preparing to Design an Effective Employee Engagement Intervention' and elsewhere, the importance of overt framing and communication of the engagement process is made.

In the case of the finance function, that meant the executive team members having to introduce the engagement process and overtly describing the nature of the invitation to participating colleagues and through their behaviour making it safe for less-senior people to get involved.

When confronted with a room full of 100-plus people, the temptation is to present and maybe ask for a few questions to check for understanding or perhaps to encourage challenge. It takes courage to engage people in a different way of participating. At first the response may well be muted until people can see that it's safe, fun and useful.

To do so means that the leader must frame the process so that they understand for themselves how much power they are willing to share, how they will govern the process and how they will instil confidence in people to pitch themselves in. As one of the chief executives I spoke to as part of the research I undertook to form this book said: 'The biggest blocker to effective employee engagement is the lack of courage of the sponsor to take risks to give the work to the people.'

Power of giving the work of change to much lower, less-politicised employees

The first steps of any engagement process are an experiment; and many remain as a single volcanic event, which is usually remembered as an activity which was never followed through. Invariably this is because, although the initial activity is described as an engagement process, the reality is often that it turns out to be more of a marketing exercise than a real sharing of power.

How many leadership events have you attended which raised the blood pressure at the time but were not followed through?

The finance story is one where the follow-through was delivered because each member of the executive team fashioned the process into their engagement process. They did so in the knowledge that in a further 90 days there would be a very public scrutiny of progress over the last 90 days; and so on.

At the end of the second 90-day period a date was fixed for a gathering of 150 finance executives with the global executive team. To reach down further into the function, five creative teams were selected from less senior levels of the function. Each was charged with bringing to life one of five strands of the strategy at the meeting:

- creating accurate and timely numbers;

- turning data into business insight;

- optimising and protecting the balance sheet;

- process efficiency;

- developing our people.

The task of 'the reach-down creative teams' was to create a 1-hour learning experience for each of the strands of the strategy which would be attended by all 150 delegates. This would mean that they have to run their experience five times providing the same learning experience each time. It also meant that they would have to explore fully what each of the strategy streams would consist of and make it interesting and accessible for the senior executives.

Given that only the headlines of the strategy streams had been developed, this involved each creative team working with sponsors for the stream on the finance executive and in effect co-creating the content of the streams. Using the creative teams was a device to accelerate the development of the change strategy. The executive team, like all such teams, were the busiest people in the function and simply could not devote the time necessary. Their younger colleagues were licensed to push the teams along.

This they did. Each team chose a different creative route to involve their audiences in the learning experience, including reworked versions of popular TV game shows such *Family Fortunes*, *Who Wants to be a Millionaire* and bespoke activities.

In a day when not a single PowerPoint slide was used, 150 people were entertained, educated and challenged to contribute to the content of the five streams in a tightly choreographed activity.

The following day was spent in natural work teams drawing up radical plans to adopt the lessons of the five change streams in each of their own regions and in devising ways to further engage their own people in these plans which were more like the experience they had just enjoyed than the usual 'death by PowerPoint'. The 90-day high-visibility events are designed to keep the pressure up, to acknowledge success and difficulties and maintain the profile of the vision process.

WHAT LESSONS CAN BE LEARNT FROM THE FINANCE STORY?

The leader of the finance function had chosen to get many change initiatives underway early in the life of the quest to turn finance around, without trying to connect them all under the heading of a grand strategy. He had waited until progress was being made and being felt and until people started to question how all the strands fitted together.

The lessons of the story include the following:

- Decide when to bring apparently disparate strands of a change together: too early and there is the danger that much seems to be promised before there is any delivery. Grand visions and strategies stated too early can give the impression that someone else is doing the work; too late and people become dispirited by the volume of new disconnected initiatives.

- Create a higher purpose and make the big idea visible: the vision process should create a higher purpose to make sense of everyone's daily work whether they are a star specialist or an administrative clerk. Most leaders soon learn how little power they really have today and sense that they cannot meet their calling without drawing on the creativity and energy of the vast majority.

- Know when to lead by consensus through an established leadership team and when to reach down: there will be times when a leadership team is the block and rather than confront it, it may help by reaching down and giving the task of driving a strategy or change to others who are less politicised.

- Give the programme a label which works: in this case calling the process a vision for finance was apposite. For others the concept of vision is tarnished. But that is not the point. The point is for the boss to have a vehicle which they can use to make sense of what may be dull, hard and perhaps unpleasant work. The vehicle might be called a strategy, a programme or an implementation plan. Finding a label which suits is important or you may put off some of the people before you start. Some people argue that labels run the risk of creating a fad. My belief is that it is hard to get people's attention, and if you really have a cause you believe in it will help to muster support.

- Action not words: whilst creating a shared story with a higher purpose is critical, if it stops there as a marketing or communication process it will have been a waste of time and the sponsor will lose credibility. The prime outcome is action which will deliver the stated aims of the vision, and that action must be driven at all levels.

- Balance local accountability with commonly applied controls: the finance story emphasises the need for the leader to engender real ownership in lower levels of management, but to do so within a framework of controls which prompt action and consistency. Engagement is not about a free-for-all democracy: it is about reaching down to implicate personally everyone who can add value.

- Take care to integrate the programme into the performance management process: so many initiatives fail because they do not feature on the carrot-and-stick process which every manager uses to target their efforts.

PART III

Engagement As Part of The Culture: Implications of Effective Engagement for Leaders, Employees and Internal Advisers

11 Creating a Climate of Engagement: Implications for Leaders and Organisational Communication

O ne of the CEOs interviewed for the research for this book said that communication sets the context or stage on which leaders engage their people. This penultimate chapter looks at the implications for leaders and organisational communication of creating a climate of effective engagement.

ANALOGIES BETWEEN POLITICAL AND BUSINESS LIFE

Politicians, especially national ones, are judged by the rest of us indirectly through the prism of owner-biased TV and print media and increasingly through the Internet where we, the ordinary citizens, have some fleeting editorial influence.

The politician as product is a construct of all their ritual media performances and citizen commentary on the Web and on the street. They are selling ideology, hopes and promises of practical action if elected. They are ambitious for themselves, their party, and their ideology and programmes – sometimes not in this order.

Effective politicians change things. Whilst the media and lobby groups can move opinion, ultimately only politicians who muster the right levels of support have the power of legislation. They are the change managers of society, and are loathed and admired in unequal measure.

Leaders and managers in business must be both the change managers and the deliverers of day-to-day performance. It's a hard balancing act. But the analogies with political life are useful. Business leaders are rarely installed to maintain the status quo. Their organisations will be in one of three situations:

- crisis of their own or someone else's making

- strategic complacency

- in transformation.

In researching the 59 organisations about approaches to employee engagement they all fell into one of these categories. Each requires a different response by the leadership. Each requires the leaders to engage their people such that they all understand the challenge the organisation faces and the role that each must fulfil. The leader must make the challenge personal. They need to recognise that few leaders can act like deities. Most must see their role as a mixture of seer and guide.

Above all the leader is there, like the politician, to bring about change. Great business leaders invent or re-invent products and markets and reform organisations.

To fulfil these roles the leader must be able to set the agenda for change, be able to get their agenda across and know which of the four approaches to engaging people and sharing power will add the value necessary.

The leader, like the politician, must recognise that they will be mostly judged indirectly on the basis of their performances in the media, over which they have some influence, and the new media, the Web and intranet, where they have much less or no influence at all, aside from the credibility of their approach.

Like it or not, leaders at any level are being constantly reviewed and voted upon. They must become and remain electable. Not too long ago that simply meant that the leader had to be a slick performer – no more. They must also understand the new rules of engagement and remember that good employees leave bosses who cannot or will not engage them sensibly in day-to-day decision making and change; and that applies as much to the call centre supervisor or airline cabin service director as much as it does the CEO.

It is not just the CEO who is the chief engagement officer, it is anyone who leads people at work.

To return to the quote at the beginning of the chapter – communication sets the context or stage on which leaders engage their people – engaging people requires much more than turbo-charged communication. It requires a shared philosophy based on an agreed definition of the term and personal capability by those who lead and manage, as well as totemic interventions which excite and temporarily lift people out of their day jobs.

But it is not or should not be framed as another form of control. The subtext of many conference speakers about employee engagement suggest that they really see employee engagement as another tool for managers to align employees by subtly making them feel some involvement, arguing that controlling or strongly influencing an employee's mindset at work is legitimate.

It may have been legitimate when employees swore loyalty to the company in exchange for security. Even where that is still the deal, it is to miss the essential point that coercion results in compliance rather than creativity. To get employees to implicate themselves and to volunteer their creativity requires leaders to take the risk of opening up the decision-making process, albeit in a well-managed way.

It is tempting to end this section reflecting on the velvet revolutions which have taken place across Eastern Europe, Africa, South America and elsewhere in which the people have always found ways to express their anger at suppression from above, and ultimately have forced their suppressors to cede and share power.

In companies, the velvet revolutionaries who feel uninvited to contribute their creativity or direct challenges to management turn to the protection of unions, resulting often in polarised and ritualised negotiations and to underground means of getting their views across. The new electronic media are already challenging the hegemony over information which corporations used to enjoy.

And of course they just vote with their feet and leave their boss in the hope of finding a culture where their ideas are welcome and sought.

DEMOGRAPHICS OF CHANGE

Good managers know how their people tick. They know what influences them. They understand the demographics of the small space of the organisation of which they are the boss.

How well do you understand the demographics of your organisation or team?

Many organisations have excellent understanding of customer demographics and may know the external political landscape when it comes to managing a process of political or regulatory persuasion. But few have a good understanding of their internal communities and their preferences and patterns. Most will, at best, be able to fish out the last internal survey of tired data which purports to track employee satisfaction.

At our consulting firm, Engage for Change, we have developed an internal demographics tool to help organisations to map their organisation so that they are in a position to make day-to-day communication relevant and to help facilitate change.

Organisations should have employee demographics data available which:

- helps them understand the community backgrounds of their employees and what those backgrounds mean in terms of how it disposes people to react and behave;

- helps them understand attitudes to work held by different groups;

- helps them understand what different groups want from work – what their idea is of the tacit contract that exists between employee and employer;

- provides an understanding of what people read, watch, listen to outside work;

- results in an understanding about which sources of influence are credible and why (peers, bosses, unions, community leaders, other companies and so on);

- provides insight into the credibility and faith people have in the communication and engagement practices of their own bosses;

- provides insight into the credibility and faith people have in the formal and informal communication processes and networks in the company.

We looked at some new approaches to measurement in Chapter 6, making the fundamental point that the traditional research industry's obsession with employee satisfaction was based on the old psychological contract referred to above, where employees swapped their loyalty to the company in exchange for security. Companies talked about their people as human assets which could be sweated but needed to be kept satisfied with the drivers which were said to foster continuing loyalty – like pay, benefits, work content, environment, communication and bosses behaviour. Employee satisfaction was the outcome being sought and as a result it reinforced the old loyalty-for-security contract which no or few organisations can deliver on any more.

Seeking to understand employee demographics rarely featured in employee satisfaction measurement. Understanding the demographics enables individual managers to relate and connect with their people and to understand what lies behind reactions from employees which may look mystifying on the surface.

Organisations should include orientations for managers which familiarises them with the demographics of their people. And managers should acquaint themselves informally with the demographics which will shape so many interactions they will have with their people.

At a formal level, good demographics will guide those managing change and post-merger integration by casting light on how people are likely to react. They will help leaders manage the relationship with any group they are engaging by giving them insight about where the group is coming from.

In fact it is amazing for me to reflect that few leaders I have worked with think much about the demographics of internal groups when preparing to interact with them. Most are pre-occupied with what they want to get across, rather than thinking about the filters, prejudices, sensitivities and 'door opening' topics which might accelerate the connection they have with the group.

By door opening I mean thinking about the spaces where people work. The view from the leader's window is out across the airport. Calls are from important people outside the company. Concerns centre on the big sweep of strategy. Down in the loaders' rest area the concerns may very well be a malfunctioning TV. In a high street retailer the concern may be the lack of tea and coffee facilities during rest breaks. Attend to the gatekeeper issues and people may become ready to listen and participate in the leader's agenda.

No astute politician would even think of launching into their pitch without touching and referencing the issues and interests of the group they are addressing – without, in other words, showing that they have bothered to listen and take action first.

Nor would they think of moving without having a clear map of which groups have the greatest influence on the voters, either positively or negatively; and among the voters, whether their disposition is positive, neutral or negative. It is more important to spend time with the neutrals and those saying they will not vote for you, than those already signed up.

In organisational change we need similar levels of demographics so that we can:

- recognise and reinforce the knowledge and confidence of those who will be advocates for the change;

- engage the neutrals in the debate particularly through the agency of colleagues who are more inclined to support;

- identify those who report themselves as being against the change because they have too little information or have the wrong information from another source of influence or are against it on ideological or intellectual grounds.

Implicating negative voices in change

We must be careful to avoid turning the antis into martyrs, and not frame them as the enemy; at least not until we have fully understood their views, respected their argument and asked ourselves whether in fact they have some good points to make.

We have to take the risk of inviting them into the process and, in the political metaphor, be willing to put ourselves up before the equivalent of the televised debate between the parties. I do not necessarily mean literally, although that may be the best solution to give confidence to the process.

Fully understanding and respecting opposing views takes time and a management view that it is better to jaw-jaw than to war-war, to paraphrase Churchill. Jaw-jaw takes time.

Stephen Windsor-Lewis, Employee Involvement and Communications Director at BAE Systems, spent the best part of 3 years locked in discussions with unions and staff groups over the vexed issue of company pensions. Like many other companies, BAE Systems are having to work out ways to meet their obligations to staff whilst at the same time meeting shareholders needs and funding research and development. The shortfalls in most company pensions is so huge that many have closed unaffordable older schemes to new staff. Aside from that, companies have a clear legal obligation to address pension deficits in full.

BAE Systems were determined to keep the scheme healthy for older and new staff alike. But to do so would mean compromise by both the company and the staff. Both would have to pay more. Of course the differences between the two sides at the outset were huge and were expressed in a lively way. And early on there was always the possibility of industrial action. But by allowing the negotiations the necessary time, an agreement was struck.

I asked Stephen if there was a magic wand solution. No, it was making the necessary time to forge a relationship which had to morph over time through distrust, disclosure and the exercise of give and take, leading to a state where very tricky negotiations could be tabled without prompting a negative emotional reaction. In other words, it was necessary to create a climate of trust in which risks could be taken and business would continue.

BAE Systems shows an alternative approach to sidelining or railroading opposition, one based on recognising that the relationship between employer and employee and employer and unions will continue after a current crisis is dealt with.

Other stories told earlier on (the logistics company in Chapter 2 and the utility company making cost cuts in Chapter 3) give similar examples of bringing all the interested and the opposing parties into the process. The advocates argue that whilst it may be tempting to crash an imposed solution through because it looks decisive and appears faster, the cultural costs are always huge.

But that is not to say that management are engaging in a free-for-all democracy. The leadership of the logistics company ran a parallel process of engaging people in the change and dealing in robust ways with the breakdown in discipline on the shop floor with a back-to-basics campaign designed to return authority for shift management, safety and well-being to the management.

In that case the supervisors had long since identified with the front line largely because management had lost the will to manage. They no longer respected management. And as the key influencing group nothing was to change until their respect had been won back.

SUPERVISORS – DAY-TO-DAY ENGAGEMENT OFFICERS

Demographics are important because they shed light on the outlook of the hidden people who lead the people every day; the supervisors, lower middle managers and team leaders.

Allan Leighton, in his role of Chairman of the UK's Royal Mail, has a mantra about employee engagement which is relevant to this section. He says: 'The what goes down, the how up.' In other words the leadership should decide what to change but the people who do the work should strongly influence and take the lead on implementation. When I interviewed him for the McKinsey and Company-sponsored engagement research he was managing the highly controversial move in the UK to cut the number of mail deliveries from two to one.

He and his executive had made the decision but that was just the start of it. It was opposed by everyone including just about the entire workforce, which is completely unionised. The unions opposed it too, seeing the move as the thin end of the wedge towards possible privatisation.

Allan Leighton had previously grown ASDA, the UK supermarket, racing past traditional competitors like Sainsbury and Safeway. It was subsequently bought by Wallmart as its UK growth vehicle. Allan brought his retail nouse and down-to-earth style of leadership to the Royal Mail. So the workforce had mixed feelings.

On the one hand here was a dynamic guy with a successful track record who spoke his mind in plain English, often from atop a box in the middle of a busy mail sorting office. On the other hand he was actually implementing the transformation which previous management teams had not dared to.

Leighton believes that much of a company's middle management obstruct radical change like the ones he had to introduce at Royal Mail. He speaks about the need to appeal direct to the posties (the nickname for the men and women who sort and deliver the mail) who know the post rounds and know best how to organise the proposed reduction so that it had least impact.

To get across his case he too applied some of the stump tactics of the politician, appearing at sorting offices during shifts and standing on whatever he could to make his pitch about the need for change and risking the derision that he often provoked. But by sticking at it other members of his audiences would appeal to their colleagues to say: 'Give the bloke a chance, he's got the guts to stand up in front of us; he could have issued commands from his office.'

By sticking at it he won the right to be heard even if the workers did not want at first to hear his message.

Having done consulting assignments at the Royal Mail I know what he means. I once witnessed a team meeting at Royal Mail in which the arrival of the manager prompted the team to stand up and turn their chairs in the opposite direction. The manager proceeded to give the briefing to the assembled group of scalps, caps, hoodies and bald heads. Not a word was exchanged at the end of his performance, aside from the profanities when he had left the room. Great theatre!

Allan Leighton gave the work of implementing the controversial reduction in mail deliveries to the people who did the work, not to scores of middle management. He knows that the real influencers are the supervisors and team leaders who are with their people all the time, not the head office managers who pop in when they have to.

Retail and service businesses have a lot to give to other sectors where the supervisory/team leader level is often the most underused and undervalued group. Yet they arguably have more influence over their staff and customers, where they are customer facing, than any other levels.

Despite that they are at the bottom of the pile for traditional briefings and most of their personal development is technical, focusing on what they have to do as opposed to how they get their people to do it.

EQUIPPING SUPERVISORS AND TEAM LEADERS TO ENGAGE THEIR OWN PEOPLE IN DAY-TO-DAY PERFORMANCE AND CHANGE

The supervisor, team leader, sergeant in the police or army, cabin service director in the air, maître d's, ward nurse and vicar are the community leaders of their part of the organisation. They are focused on delivering the organisation's service or product day in and day out. They deliver against prescribed or tacit standards of service with clearly identified levels of personal discretion, which vary from none to considerable depending on the organisation and service or product being delivered. In other words, for most of their day they are repeating variations of the same task.

The organisation needs this consistency and often the customers expect it.

Customers come to expect clotted cream tea in business class on BA. Medical procedures are specified procedures; introducing a catheter requires the procedure to be followed. The vicar has a routine and a dogma to follow. Jean Claude, the maître d' at top chef Gordon Ramsay's Hospital Road restaurant in London's Chelsea, is one of the most charming men on the planet, but behind the performance lies a clearly specified service proposition and fiery but inspiring boss!

And of course many people delivering service day to day derive all the satisfaction that they need from the work they do. A good cabin service director on a BA or Virgin aeroplane enjoys nothing better than delivering a good service and having someone acknowledge it.

Good supervisors may be well trained in getting their teams to deliver the specified day-to-day product but two apparently identical experiences may be very different for customers on the receiving end. Mood, tone, curiosity and energy are hard to prescribe, yet it is these aspects of service delivery which raise a service experience from 'it ticked all the boxes' to 'wow that was special'.

On one occasion my wife had a slipped disc and we exchanged air miles for first-class BA tickets to the Caribbean. Outbound was a delight; the return was dismal. Outwardly all was as it should be. The difference lay in the mood, tone and the lack of energy and curiosity of the crew; and in both cases the cabin service director was responsible. They are the conductors, the choreographers of the people under their spell in the small spaces where most people work. Very often they are the embodiment of the brand. They are the law and they are mummy, daddy, friend and colleague. They are the organisation.

Everyone has their off days, but the point is that the supervisor has it in their power to enable their teams to perform. The leisure company case in Chapter 8 illustrates how one company invested in their managerial and supervisory levels in a strategy to drive up service levels. The objective of the company called Obsession was to put them in charge of devising breakthrough customer service improvements which could be achieved with the resources already at their disposal and which would require investment.

The CEO of the leisure company knew that a centrally imposed service strategy would be complied with but not fully owned by those closest to customers, but that a strategy which the 2000 managers and supervisors and the whole company had a hand in creating, would result in a popular movement characterised by energy. He had recently announced the best margins in the industry and to retain this distinction would require the engagement of everyone.

He had also recognised that it was the supervisory layer which held the key to influencing the rest of the population.

He was thinking like a political strategist.

CEO AS CHIEF ENGAGEMENT OFFICER

That CEO knew that when it came to fermenting a velvet revolution in his organisation he had to set and reward the right role models of employee engagement. The trouble is that being the CEO he has to make the right role model visible through layers of the organisation. Regardless of the size of the organisation it is possible to categorise the population into five types of actor. Each has a part to play in creating a climate of engagement. The five groups are characterised in the Figure 11.1.

The categorisation is offered as a way of thinking about the demographics of the organisation and as a prompt to target the right groups when planning to engage the organisation in raising performance or a change or transformation process.

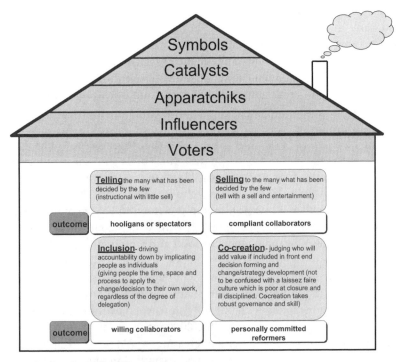

Source: John Smythe and McKinsey & Company

Figure 11.1   Five types of actor in an organisation

Symbols

At the top of the 'house' are the Symbols. Symbols are the senior leaders who are seen so infrequently by many that they could also be called 'ghosts', on account of their ethereal presence. Symbols are responsible for higher-order drivers or influences on people's views and behaviour like:

* vision

* values

* ethics

* strategy

* brand.

169

Symbols are experienced by most staff indirectly through ritual processes – large gatherings, road shows, electronic communication including Web TV and electronic meetings. Sometimes they make ritual site visits.

Occasionally they are spotted in the canteen or the corridor and lift. Symbols rely on assumed power to instigate change which they must largely exercise through the Catalysts. They have real power over the Catalysts but usually Symbols need to work through the Catalysts to get to the Voters.

Catalysts

The second group are the Catalysts. They are the business unit head, the operations director, the country chief, the head of a function. They are closer to the Voters and have real power over them. Their responsibility is to make strategy happen, to drive day-to-day business performance and to lead change. They are much more visible and physically present than Symbols.

Their engagement role model will be felt, experienced, talked about and copied much more than the distant role model of the Symbols. The Symbols rely upon and must engage the Catalysts or fail.

Apparatchiks

The Apparatchiks are Allan Leighton's impervious marzipan layer of middle managers, who are the source of frustration of so many Symbols and Catalysts. But when engaging the organisation they need to be enfranchised or circumvented. They are both the source of stability and can see themselves as the protector against rash change. They may have huge sway over the Influencers.

Influencers

The Influencers are the supervisors and team leaders who lead and manage the people every day. They are the most under-utilised asset in the organisation and the most influential on the perceptions and experience of work of those they supervise.

They are usually only seen in the context of the day job whereas they have huge potential as agents and role models for change. Think of them as the grass roots organisations of political parties. The CEO wishing to accelerate change should reach down to this group both in planning engagement interventions, like the ones for the leisure company in Chapter 8 and for the finance example in Chapter 10, and in broadening the job role development process to equip them to understand and carry out their engagement role every day and in times of change.

Voters

I have made much of the political analogy, perhaps too much. My point is that leaders and managers at any level must compete for the ear, interest and retention of their employees. It is worth remembering that unions use the term 'members' inferring a community of interest. The emerging psychological contract between employee and employer is very different to the cradle-to-grave model of former times.

Figure 11.2, used earlier, is a reminder of some of the shifts in the employer/ employee relationship.

The concepts will be familiar to readers as many other authors have written about them. Charles Handy, for example, encapsulated the idea of portfolio careers.

The shift adds up to a workforce which is much more mobile, sceptical of the reliability of employers and more interested in developing personal employability by grazing skills from employer to employer.

The new employee is aware of the drivers provided by the employer which engage them and will vote with their feet and move on when those drivers no longer add value to them or they are in conflict with them. As we noted in Chapter 6 on measurement, organisations need to distinguish between categories of drivers which the employees will be voting on. Figure 11.2 is a reminder.

Of the three categories, the first two – instrumental and cultural – are within the immediate jurisdiction of senior leadership, the executive cadre. Workplace drivers, which are influencing the vast mass of employees, are beyond the immediate control of top leadership. For most employees they are delivered by their bosses, who are typically the Influencers.

They are the key determinants of the real culture on the ground.

Cradle to grave	⇒	portfolio careers
Loyalty	⇒	transactional relationship
Dependence	⇒	independence
'Our human resources'	⇒	creative talent on loan
Employees	⇒	citizens
Big institutions	⇒	my own company
Command and control	⇒	well governed inclusivity
CEO = GOD	⇒	CEO = Guide
I left the company	⇒	I left my boss
Local community	⇒	workplace communities

Figure 11.2   Shifts in employer/employee relationships

What drivers do you need to focus on to deliver a distinct customer offer and a compelling place to work?

Figure 11.3   Drivers to deliver a distinct customer offer and a compelling place to work

GROWING ENGAGEMENT CAPABILITY

Growing engagement capability begins with understanding the combination of drivers or influences which retain the best people and enable them to be the most productive. In Chapter 6 I argued that this combination of drivers will be unique to the organisation and the situation it finds itself in (strategic complacency, crisis or transformation).

Armed with a picture of influential drivers, the organisation needs to align its goal setting and development programmes. Learning about the organisation's philosophy and approach to employee engagement should be included in recruitment, orientation and capability development, and form a prerequisite for any team leader, supervisor, manager and leader.

The syllabus for employee engagement should cover:

- the organisation's philosophy about employee engagement;

- the complete decision cycle; the role of engagement and communication planning in improving decision making and execution (see Chapter 5 for detail) and the impact of personal communication performance styles on the outcome of interactions between the boss and their people;

- knowing what being a good interpersonal communicator actually does and dispelling some common assumptions.

And as a reminder of what being a chief engagement officer means:

- advocating the company's vision;

- focusing people on the right work;

- pastoral care – knowing and delivering what engages their people;

- power sharing – considering who to engage in decision making and execution and governing it well;

- authentic presence – having insight and exercising discipline about personal communication style and tone;

- attractive values including fairness and transparency;

- (and is good at the day job).

This section concludes with a look at the false assumptions about what a good communicator does and the ten behaviours of the good communicator.

The six false assumptions about leaders who 'communicate well':

- are charismatic leaders who present well;

- are born, not made;

- are gods who have all the answers;

- withhold bad news to keep morale up;

- think that force of personality will persuade people;

- makes everyone feel as if they are involved.

The biggest false assumption about leaders who communicate well is that that they must be type A personalities with great presence who can sell ice to Eskimos.

It is a false assumption because it is based on the assumption that it is one-way traffic. This style is just one of the 14 identified in the communication styles typography in Chapter 5.

So how does a good communicator actually behave? They:

- know that they can't achieve their vision and targets without engaging the right people. They consciously consider who to involve in decision forming to drive value and 'stickiness' in execution;

- understand that communication usually takes place within the context of a relationship where past experiences will influence success;

- recognise that secrecy destroys credibility. They know that once they start saying 'what's our line?' on a topic that the people will sense the economy. They know that leaders live in a goldfish bowl visible to all;

- communicate decisions as they are made, distinguishing them from work in progress;

- plan the engagement and communication from the perspective of the other party;

- make the invitation to participate very clear and allow people to see the impact of their contribution;

- show how initiatives are connected to the big picture;

- understand the demographics of the implicated groups;

- are aware of and adapt their personal communication styles to the situation;

- know that listening means saying little and being very interested in what the other party is saying.

CHANGING THE DNA OF INTERNAL COMMUNICATION FROM COERCION TO INCLUSION

This book started by briefly tracing the history of internal communication noting that it is in danger of becoming an overused and corrupted tool of the command-and-control leadership style. Many internal communicators find themselves to be little more than post hoc sense makers running behind their bosses trying to craft coherent messages.

But some have managed to change the DNA from message making and coercion to inclusion. Take the statement of purpose for the communication team of a global company shown in Figure 11.4.

This charter marked the beginning of a journey for the communicators from being the tactical message makers, the 'medic', to being the internal 'adviser', who facilitates their business partners into factoring the human consequences and opportunities into decisions and plans.

This shift is represented in Figure 11.5.

The challenge for organisations is to reflect on the DNA of their communication resource and, if it is stuck in messaging and cascading at staff, to effect a transition to an inclusive advisory approach suggested in the charter above. The consequences of failing to take action are that employees may experience more engaging behaviour from their bosses only to have it confounded by old style *tell* and *sell* formal communication which smacks of hype and economy and damages the credibility of management.

Bosses need to know that their internal advisers are part of the solution, not part of the problem; communicators also need to know if they are part of the problem or the opportunity.

We will:

Challenge our business partners to consider the people implications of decisions, plans, strategies and change programmes in order to:

- improve decisions and content of change and strategy;
- drive faster and more sustainable implementation;
- stimulate the creativity of our people for the benefit of the business and to create a better place to work.

Interpret business plans, decisions, strategies and change into understandable stories and news which are clear and compelling.

Shift from a messaging approach to communication to an outcomes-based approach to planning communication, focusing our internal clients on thinking through – with us – what we want to achieve as a result of communication:

- cognitively, what we want people to understand;
- affectively, what we want people to feel;
- behaviourally, what we want people to do.

Distinguish between communication – setting the context/creating the backstory/the news – and engagement, in which we help to design programmes and interventions which involve the right groups in contributing to decision making, strategies and change.

Coach our leaders towards becoming communication and engagement role models.

We will continue to master all the foundation skills of communicators and the new skills of employee engagement and be masters of emerging technology which provide unparalleled opportunities to connect and engage all our stakeholders, internally and externally.

We will become excellent facilitators to enable us to lead confidently our discussions with our business partners.

We will identify and work and where appropriate lead cross-functional groups on projects such as brand, communication planning and employee engagement.

We will help our cousins in leadership development to build communication and employee engagement capability into people development programmes.

Figure 11.4   A global company's new charter for communication

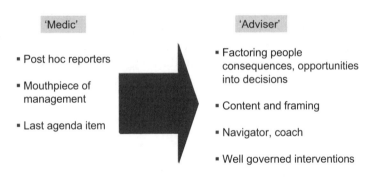

Source: *SmytheDorwardLambert*

Figure 11.5   Challenges of the shift

Figure 11.6 shows the different roles that can be adopted.

The model is Maslovian in the sense that the lower-order activities ascend to higher-value roles for communicators. Communicators need to be familiar with the lower-order activity before ascending to the roles of activist or adviser. Use the diagram to assess the current level of your communication team by estimating the amount of time spent in each role. Develop a transition plan based on the assessment.

The first step in building the transition is to develop a charter or vision for communication, one which is rooted in the needs of the business over the next 18 months to 2 years.

The next step is to review every aspect of communication activity to determine how the aims of the vision will be reflected in the day-to-day work of the communicators.

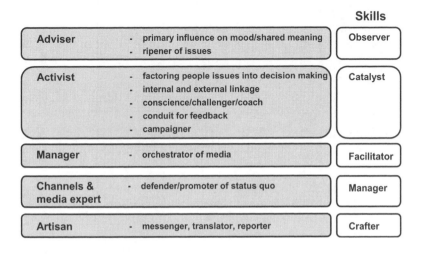

Source: *SmytheDorwardLambert*

Figure 11.6   Spectrum of communication roles

Figure 11.7 which follows is an attempt to capture every element and activity undertaken by communicators. At Engage for Change we use this diagram as the basis for a workshop in which we take each box and undertake a from–to exercise to help the communicators chart the changes they will need to make to bring their activities into line with the charter or vision for communication.

We also acknowledge that this diagram originated at our former consultancy SmytheDorwardLambert.

EPILOGUE TO CHAPTER 11

If I had the opportunity to work on one of these approaches to creating a sustainable climate of engagement it would involve focusing on the supervisor's perceptions of what leading people means in terms of giving

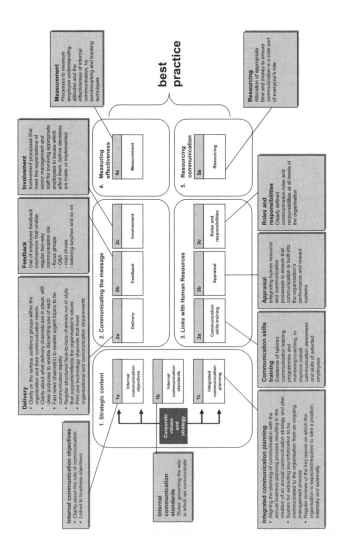

Source: SmytheDorwardLambert and Engage for Change

Figure 11.7   Elements of a communication strategy

their people the opportunity to contribute to day-to-day decision making and change.

In the final chapter I hand over to academic Johanna Fawkes to take you on a whirlwind tour of recent writing (in 2005/2006) about employee engagement which may whet your appetite to explore this emerging topic more.

12 Employee Engagement – A Review of the Literature

Johanna Fawkes

The aim of this chapter is to provide an overview of recent research (largely between 2000 and 2005) in the field of employee engagement. It brings together findings from a variety of sources including major research projects funded by global consultancies, independent research organisations, general and academic books and papers.

It cannot hope to be comprehensive but should offer readers insight into current thinking in the field and possibly suggest further reading for those wishing to investigate the subject more deeply.

The content was gathered using mainstream search engines (primarily Google and www.findarticles.com), an academic online library (www.questia.com) and a variety of books, articles and proprietary research reports. All sources are clearly identified and there is a reference list at the end of the chapter. The material was then analysed to identify common themes and threads – including contradictions.

Because employee engagement is a fairly recent development of older theories of motivation and communication, there is not yet a body of critical reflection available, as most authors are participants in the business of engagement rather than dispassionate critics. As the Institute for Employment Studies (Robinson et al. 2004, 1) says: 'For such a well-used and popular term, engagement has surprisingly little associated research.' Their review of literature also found few academic studies, with the bulk of the material emanating from consultancies and survey houses. The most comprehensive review of the research into links between employee attitudes and performance comes from the Work Foundation's (2005) literary review (www.theworkfoundation.com/pdf/Literary_review.pdf). The range of sources for this chapter are outlined below.

This chapter starts with a thematic analysis of approaches to the concept of employee engagement, in an attempt to draw out underlying assumptions or priorities in each study/research project. It suggests that employee engagement programmes often draw on psychological or sociological theories and that some emphasise the business case as the primary motivation; others focus on the needs of employees. These categories are not exclusive but an aid to exploring the subject area.

This discussion also raises a few questions about the assumptions and implications of current practices. For example, while the case between positive attitudes and productivity does seem proven, there is little reflection on the ethics of 'engineering' the emotions of a workforce, either by selective recruitment or engagement programmes. Of course, happy motivated groups of employees must be preferable to disgruntled, alienated workers for all concerned. Yet, perhaps perversely, the rights of an employee to be fed up but still do a decent job seem worth defending; the echoes of Big Brother can be heard under some of these texts and this chapter tries to amplify such concerns.

This chapter then sets out the main measures, dimensions and driver analyses offered by the main consultancies and survey houses in the field for comparison and interest.

Finally, the conclusion draws out the key observations emerging from the research.

SOURCES OF CURRENT RESEARCH

Most of the research material covered in this chapter is post 2000 and comes from the following sources:

- *commercial organisations which offer surveys and/or engagement programmes*, such as Towers Perrin (2004) which interviewed 15 000 European workers in public and private organisations in six countries; International Survey Research (ISR) (2004) which surveyed ten large economies, 160 000 employees, hundreds of companies across industries; and Gallup, who arguably started the trend with their late-1990s survey of 1 million employees and 80 000 managers worldwide;

- *management consultants*, such as Accenture, McKinsey & Company and Watson Wyatt who have developed their own approaches to employee engagement;

- *independent research bodies*, such as Melcrum and the Work Foundation, which are funded by subscription and produce a variety of publications and reports, though they may also raise revenue through conferences and workshops;

- *individual consultants*, such as Kowalski or Welbourne, who run companies offering advice but also write academic or professional papers in a variety of journals;

- *academics*, who have written books and/or articles on the subject of employee engagement, usually from a human resources perspective.

There is an overlap between these categories; several of the individual consultants are also PhDs with academic histories or current university positions. Nevertheless, there is a marked difference in tone between these sources: those in the first category are upbeat and clear about the positive impact of engagement on the bottom line and the universal applicability of their particular model or approach; the independent bodies and academics tend to be more reflective; the survey organisations and individual consultants tend to be prescriptive (of their own remedies); the impartial bodies and academics are more critical of the theories and practices involved.

However, the largest-scale research has been undertaken by the commercial organisations, and their findings, such as the discrepancy between engagement levels in the USA and Asia and those in Europe, particularly France, are often extremely interesting and relevant to the wider discussion of employee engagement.

The next section compares the different approaches to employee engagement taken by these organisations and in particular examines the problems of defining the field.

DEFINITIONS AND APPROACHES

When Melcrum (2005) began their interviews with 1000 managers who have run engagement programmes across the world, they found a host of differing, even conflicting, views about what employee engagement was. Some described it as a programme of activity, others as a set of ideas; some thought it was just internal communications repackaged to sell surveys, others thought the survey *was* the engagement; some focused on employee performance; others on internal branding. There was also confusion about whether employees were being encouraged to engage with their company, their boss or their job.

As the Melcrum report emphasises, this matters. Lack of clarity about the goals of an enterprise must undermine its effectiveness, as any strategist will attest.

Analysis of the definitions and approaches suggests they can be grouped as follows:

- concepts which originate from psychological theories;
- concepts based on sociological or cultural ideas;

- management-centred perspectives;

- employee-centred perspectives.

These categories are not mutually exclusive, of course: most management-centred approaches explore employee attitudes to understand the engagement process, for example. But they help illustrate the roots of employee engagement thinking in classic social science theory and also highlight the question of who is engagement for.

Psychological approaches

Many of the key concepts in employee engagement have their origins in theories from social psychology, concerning motivation and attitudes. The classic theories of employee motivation, such as McGregor (1960), Hertzberg (1966) and Alderfer (1969) are seen by Frank et al. (2004) as providing the roots for employee engagement. One can go back to Maslow's (1943) powerfully influential Hierarchy of Needs pyramid, which identified the escalating needs of human beings from pure survival, through social and family ties to self-realisation at the highest, most spiritual level. This has been updated by Andrew Brown of Mercer Delta Counselling who has adapted Maslow's model to describe the stages of employee engagement, according to Melcrum (2005), rising from satisfaction through commitment to engagement.

Another key concept adapted from social psychology includes the 'psychological contract', a term first used in the 1960s but which has gained currency in the past 20 years. It is defined by Guest and Conway (2002) as 'the perceptions of the two parties, employee and employer, of what their mutual obligations are towards each other'. The old deal was the social contract whereby an employee received wages, fair conditions and job security for a decent day's work. Then the psychological contract described the exchange of loyalty for security; now it covers a wider range of behaviours and attitudes from employer to employee and vice versa, with increasing emphasis on issues like employability, empowerment and work/life balance. (For more information see the CIPD factsheet, *Managing the Psychological Contract*, revised January 2006, from www.cipd.co.uk.)

Other psychologically based approaches examine the attitudes of workers towards their work, workplace and employer and characterise them accordingly. One example is Quirke's (2002) matrix of employees as either 'unguided missiles' (willing to help but unclear about direction); 'slow burners' (unwilling to help and unclear about direction); 'refuseniks' (unwilling to help but clear about direction); and finally 'hot shots' (willing to help and clear about direction). An MCA/MORI research study from the late 1990s (Thomson and Hecker 2000) suggests that 14 per cent of UK workers could be called unguided missiles (they used the term 'loose cannon'); 39 per cent fit the slow burner (or 'weak links') group; with 20 per cent acting as refuseniks or saboteurs; and 37 per cent as hotshots or champions (some crossover apparent from the total).

The International Survey Research (ISR) approach to employee engagement clearly draws on social psychological research into attitudes as their model uses the dimensions of cognition (thoughts), affect (feelings) and behaviour to map the attitudes of employees. This tripartite understanding of attitudes was developed by Rosenberg and Hovland (1960) but it does not address the relationships between these elements – unlike the Theory of Reasoned Action (Fishbein and Azjen 1980) or Festinger's (1957) Cognitive Dissonance, for example, which seek to explain the complex and hard-to-predict links between attitudes, beliefs and behaviour. A more useful approach might be Fishbein and Azjen's (1975) earlier Expectancy Value theory which suggests that attitudes are formed when a belief about an object, person or organisation is confirmed or disconfirmed, as for example when trust is rewarded or abused (see also Fawkes 2006). In other words, it is not always clear why one psychological model has been deployed rather than another, though ISR state a preference for this model because it is contemporaneous – with all the elements occurring at once – rather than sequential (private correspondence, 2007).

Other examples of the use of psychological approaches include academics Welbourne and Gubman, both of whom are also consultants in the field of employee engagement. Welbourne employs role theory in her work with clients to understand motivation and employee engagement, according to one of her papers (2003), which would seem to be based on Bandura's Social Learning Theory (1971), though this is not acknowledged. This suggests that we learn how to behave in situations by watching those around us and selecting available behavioural roles. She identifies the roles relevant to engagement as escalating through:

- job holder
- team member
- entrepreneur
- career
- organisation member.

The first does the minimum to keep the job; the last works to help the company regardless of their job description. Welbourne also emphasises the importance of employees owning the process and argues against letting corporate directives dominate engagement.

Gubman (2004), on the other hand, appears more closely identified with the management perspective (see also below). He draws on the 'Big Five' personality traits (McCrae and Costa 2002): extraversion v introversion; conscientiousness v unidirectedness; agreeableness v antagonism; emotional stability v neuroticism; openness v closed to experience. These traits were adapted for business by Howard and Howard (2001) to create a behavioural matrix and Gubman's workshop-based research located 'passionate employees' on this map. They were found to:

- be relatively extraverted (or ambiverted – able to work in teams or alone, as required)

- be goal-driven

- employ variety of interpersonal styles

- handle change well

- like the new and different in their work.

This looks like a description of the 'hot shot' employees identified by Quirke (2002) above. But this, like some other psychological approaches, seems very instrumental, serving a means not an end. The diagnosis is a test to help the employer recruit – and reject – for passion rather than other qualities, though Gubman does not ask what an organisation consisting of passionate employees might look like or even if this is desirable – might it not be like living in a soap opera? There is an undercurrent of emotional coercion in Gubman's approach which can also be found in the selective use of psychology to bolster management goals (see also criticism of management approaches below).

This brings us to work on emotional labour (Yeomans 2005) which describes the degree of emotional presentation or 'face work' (Goffman 1959) required in the workplace. An influential book by Hochschild, first published in 1983 (2nd edition 2003), *The Managed Heart; Commercialization of Human Feeling*, estimated that a third of US workers had jobs which subjected them to high demands for emotional labour which was then used for commercial gain. Maintaining a gap between what is actually felt and what *should* be felt, according to 'display rules' can give rise to deep alienation/burnout over the long term, according to Hochschild's research with Delta Airlines. Gubman's approach, outlined above, might risk this damage, in seeking to commodify passion as a condition of employment.

Social psychology theories have proved rich pickings for those developing approaches to employee engagement. There is, however, as Hochschild suggests, a danger that selective emphasis on employee attitudes will focus on the ideas that favour management rather than employee interests (see 'Employee-centred approaches' below).

Sociological approaches

Another cluster of employee engagement models are based on sociological and/or cultural concepts. One of the most notable is the research into social networks conducted (Lesser and Prusak 2004) on behalf of IBM.

Unlike some of the above-mentioned surveys which seek to ascertain the attitudes of individual workers, this research looked at how groups behave. Although the sources are not explained in the book, the concept of social capital was developed by a number of sociologists, most notably Bourdieu (1984) and Bourdieu and Waquant (1992), and has come to mean the value individuals, groups and organisations derive from their social networks. Social capital is also referred to in The Work Foundation report (2005) into company performance, but the report suggests that British companies have failed to understand the role of social capital, relationship theory and network analysis, and that this failure of understanding is a contributing factor to low engagement levels.

Social network analysis, in turn, draws on sociological studies from the 1950s (Barnes 1954 and Bott 1955). It allows maps to be created showing how relationships flow or stall between individuals, groups and organisations, internally and externally. The IBM approach explains how social network analysis was used to generate four dimensions through which knowledge moves within networks: awareness (that the knowledge exists), access (to the knowledge itself), engagement (willingness of knowledge holders to work with knowledge-seekers) and safety (trust, freedom from fear of ridicule and so on). It is worth mentioning that informal networks are increasingly seen as key to how knowledge *really* moves inside an organisation.

The central concepts of networks draws on Castells' (2000) idea of 'a network society' of fluctuating cooperation and flexible partnerships between employee and employer groups replacing the rigid hierarchies of earlier epochs. There is less analysis of how this might affect individual workers but Castells argued that the 'the traditional form of work, based on full-time employment, clear-cut occupational assignments, and a career pattern over the life cycle is being slowly but surely eroded away' (p. 268).

Most writing on employee engagement takes this shift in working life as a given. It is also worth noting that government research, such as the Department for Trade and Industry (DTI) investigations into employees and employers attitudes to the work/life balance use sociological research methods. The DTI/Work Foundation report (2005) *People, Strategy, Performance* covers many of the issues that provide the social, political and economic context to employee engagement: business performance measures; issues of attraction and retention; the impact of the knowledge economy and intangible assets. The question of demographics and the impact of an ageing workforce are also considered by Frank et al. (2004) and Jamrog (2004), both of which stress the urgency with which employers need to address the changing social environment.

The social context for employee engagement is also considered in the links between engagement activities and corporate social responsibility (CSR).

The Melcrum report makes specific mention of the Corporate Citizenship Company report, *Good companies, Better employees* (2003) which worked with MORI to survey 975 nationally representative UK employees into feelings about effects of corporate community involvement (CCI). It found a strong link between CCI activities and positive attitudes towards the employing organisation, and 70 per cent of employees surveyed expressed pride in their organisation's ethical stance. This echoes The Work Foundation's *Ethical Employee* report (2001), which also linked CSR activities to employee loyalty.

Another definition which locates employee engagement in the social sphere comes from Smythe (2005) who describes it as 'a social process, considered or accidental, by which leaders and employers become personally implicated in the performance of their own team in the context of contribution to wider organisational change, strategy, transformation, operational movement or day-to-day performance'). The power sharing elements of his approach are described later in this chapter and elsewhere, of course, in this book.

There is probably scope for greater use of sociological approaches, including cultural theories, to understand employee engagement. There has been considerable discussion about corporate culture in the context of organisational communication and change management, but less in the field of employee engagement. Kowalski (2002) and The Work Foundation report (2005) talk about the corporate culture and its impact on encouraging or discouraging employee engagement (see also under 'Drivers', below) but it is a dimension missing from many of the other texts covered here.

One cultural commentator worth exploring is Hofstede (1991), who has suggested four dimensions of national cultures and linked them to leadership issues:

- *Power distance* – how wide is the power gap between leaders and subordinates?

- *Uncertainty avoidance* – how anxious is the society and what measures does it take to reduce or manage uncertainty?

- *Individualism v collectivism* – is the society organised around the rights and interests of individuals or groups?

- *Masculinity v femininity* – is competition valued over cooperation, for example?

These ideas seem highly relevant to the questions raised in discussion of employee engagement, and in particular the role of leaders. However such debates in the existing literature are mostly structured around management theory.

Management-led approaches

Many of the leading advocates of employee engagement programmes address the needs of management above all, concentrating on the business case for engagement programmes. There are good reasons for this: firstly, the evidence that the role of leadership is crucial to successful engagement, so management must buy in to engagement; secondly the programmes are expensive so management must also literally buy them. There is a danger that the combination of factors can lead to top-down, corporate-led engagement plans, but the work done by the large consultancies undoubtedly repays closer examination. Moreover, many stress the need for management to be more responsive to and engaged with their employees, not merely for the employees to line up behind them.

Probably the most influential of the management-led approaches is the Gallup research of the late 1990s which resulted in the book, *First, Break All the Rules* (Buckingham and Vosburgh 1999). This arose from a worldwide survey of one million employees and 80 000 managers. When the authors analysed the results they identified the elements that separated high- and low-performing businesses (using a wide range of measures, including customer satisfaction, to determine performance regardless of sector). This led to the famous 12-statement framework where those businesses with strong support for statements such as *I know what is expected of me at work*, *I know my opinions count at work*, and, controversially, *I have a best friend at work* were consistently shown to outperform their peers, including separate branches of the same company.

Further research, case-studies and follow-up surveys confirmed the results, suggesting, as they put it, that 'people leave managers not companies.'

The levels of engagement were mapped in a series of global studies, which found about 20 per cent of the workforce was engaged (more in the US and some Asian countries), less than 20 per cent were actively disengaged (that figure was higher in France) and the majority of workers were between these two poles. The UK study of 2003 suggested that disengaged workers had higher absence and sickness records and their cost to the UK economy would fund the NHS for a year.

This approach – survey followed by cost/benefit analysis – is common to employee engagement programme vendors like Towers Perrin, Accenture and ISR, for example. Towers Perrin mapped employees worldwide in 2003 and 2004 to ascertain why people join an organisation (attraction) and why they stay (retention). They found that employee attitudes were linked to economic forces and varied according to the social contexts, but that 'Highly engaged people outperform those less engaged, leading to measurable differences in company performance. Engaged employees are also far more likely to stay with their employer. Failing to engage people … is tantamount to approving lower performance and higher staff turnover.' (Towers Perrin 2004, 4)

ISR research in 2003 also linked engagement with financial performance, showing that 'a 5 per cent increase in positive employee attitudes was reliably linked to a 2.1 per cent increase in ... sales performance' (Harding, *European Quality*, date n/k). The financial interests of the employer are clear from their definition of engagement as 'a process by which an organisation increases the commitment and contribution of its employees to achieve superior business results'. The methods by which an organisation can attempt to increase another's commitment are outlined in the next section, but it does imply that commitment can be managed, even manipulated, rather than won. Indeed the title of the ISR 2005 White Paper, *Creating Competitive Advantage from Your Employees,* also suggests an instrumental approach to the workforce. Yet the studies of emotional labour referred to earlier suggest that if management-led approaches become coercive, employees will experience increased stress and alienation.

Accenture measures engagement according to the degree to which employees are satisfied, understand their organisation's strategic goals, contribute to achieving those goals, are aligned with corporate values and stay in the job. All of these measures are employer benefits, of course. However, their research also found most respondents evaluated themselves and their organisation as poor achievers in these areas, suggesting much work to be done on achieving these goals (see below for implementing engagement strategies).

Another research project which stressed the cost to the country of disengaged workers was produced by The Work Foundation as part of a DTI investigation into engagement. The 2005 report, *Cracking the Performance Code,* analysed 3000 UK companies over a year to see what factors might account for high/ low performance, including share price data, case-study analysis and previous research. This found that the top third companies outperform the remainder by £1600 per worker per annum. It goes on to identify how the added value is derived (see 'Drivers' below) and its impact on gross profits.

Although the Gubman (2004) paper on passionate employees was discussed under the psychological approach sections, it could also be seen as a management-led approach to engagement, as it seeks to establish a particular criterion – passion – as the basis for recruitment policies. Interestingly, Shaffer (2004) suggests that engagement policies need not be directed at all employees, but should be targeted at those individuals who make the most significant impact on an organisation's performance: 'Getting to 100 per cent engaged may require an investment for which there's no return ... By focusing on the critical few people, often less than ten per cent of the entire workforce, companies can make significant performance improvements.'

Some of the management myths about engagement are dispelled by Frank et al. (2004) who point out that for all the concern with measuring retention and attraction as demonstrators of engagement, external economic factors may influence job movements more than engagement policies or practices. They also point out that retention may include 'deadwood' employees and that highly engaged employees may not stay with the firm because they are eager for new experiences.

This paper also highlights the work on the role of the front-line leader as described by a range of scholars, all of which confirms the importance of line managers and senior leaders in determining employees' attitudes to their company and their work. For example, according to Hudson Research (2004) a third of employees rate their bosses as fair or poor. (See also the discussion on leadership under 'Role of Leaders'.)

Many of the above approaches suggest that employees can be adapted to the organisation's goals and values in order, ultimately, to increase profits. None of them suggest this is easy, but they do suggest it can be done. The next section looks at research which keeps its focus on employee benefits and motives. It is important to note that these categories do not represent opposite poles – clearly management initiatives to improve employee motivation are mutually beneficial. Indeed it is a central argument of employee engagement that managers need to pay more attention to employees' psychological and emotional needs in order to improve their overall performance. The distinction lies perhaps in the language used and the emphasis on whose interests predominate. Shifting the focus does reveal some useful insights into different approaches to engagement.

Employee-centred approaches

It is notable that one of the authors of the pioneering Gallup research, Marcus Buckingham, has since expressed concern that employee engagement has become a systems- rather than people- centred activity (Buckingham and Vosburgh 2001). This paper argues that HR has got sidetracked in programmes and systems and forgotten its mission to 'help one particular person increase his or her performance'.

In particular, the reliance of HR professionals on competences is criticised, a view supported by research from New Zealand (Markus et al. 2005). Competence-based programmes tend to encourage a uniform approach to people and pay undue attention to fixing weaknesses. This contradicts the findings from Gallup that excellent leaders all solve problems differently: instead of engineering identical responses to work demands, individuals should be encouraged to develop their own responses. Buckingham and Vosburgh suggest engagement and retention programmes should be based simply on:

- skill (ability to do teachable tasks)

- knowledge (both factual and experiential)

- talent ('recurring patterns of thought, feeling or behaviour that can be productively applied').

This last concept is seen as essential to creative development and seven steps are suggested for building a 'talented organisation'.

The IES study (Robinson et al. 2004, p.9) is clear that engagement is two way: 'organisations must work to engage the employee', which offers a different emphasis to some of the approaches outlined above. They define engagement as 'a concept held by the employee towards the organisation and its values. An engaged employee is aware of the business context and works with colleagues to improve performance within the job for the benefit of the organisation. The organisation must work to develop and nurture engagement, which requires a two-way relationship between employer and employee.'

Their 2003 survey of 10 000 NHS employees used the 12 statements approach developed by Gallup and found that engagement levels varied according to age, ethnicity, managerial role and length of service. Accidents or injury at work impacted engagement negatively; having a personal development plan, positively.

Smythe also places employees at the centre of the process, as agents not objects of change. He stresses the issue of accountability in Chapter 3 and the approach to engagement embraces power sharing as a central concept:

> *Employee engagement requires leaders at every level to share their power with their people. To drive the best results means inviting the people who deliver the end result to contribute to: everyday decision making; vision, strategy and implementation; crises, change and transformation; brand and service. In other words it means including people in the decision-making process, not communicating with them after decisions have been made. (www.engageforchange.com)*

His four styles of engagement encourage employers to move away from diktat and towards informed participation.

Perhaps the employee-centred approach is best summed up by Kowalski's (2002) definition: 'Employee engagement is the degree to which individuals are personally committed to helping an organisation by doing a better job than required to hold the job.'

Kowalski uses the term 'discretionary effort' to describe the difference between an employee merely doing their job and one who is engaged. This reminds one that the initiative to exceed the requirements of the job is volunteered not coerced.

Summary

The different interpretations of employee engagement offered above can be multiplied almost ad infinitum, according to the Melcrum report (2005) which asked 1000 managers what it meant to them. The answers involved practically everything, all at once. The report suggests that this lack of clarity in understanding what employee engagement actually is threatens the development of engagement itself, as:

- It will always remain at a theoretical level within the organisation.

- There will be conflicts within the design team due to different interpretations.

- Messages will be inconsistent, preventing ownership from taking place.

MEASUREMENT AND DRIVERS

Data collection

The previous section looked at the different perspectives and priorities adopted by a variety of researchers and survey vendors. The next part aims to provide an overview of the tools they use to measure, what they actually measure and how they propose rectifying problems found. This section is less analytical, and simply offers descriptions of the key measures used by researchers and consultants. These are of course heavily influenced by the preferred approach of each organisation, and most of the major survey groups have their own set of tools which are not directly comparable. Most survey organisations gather a range of data then map them according to a particular approach to identify the 'drivers' of engagement, those factors which appear to provide the critical difference between the engaged and disengaged workforce.

Drivers are discussed in more detail below but first it is worth noting that data-gathering tools tend to fall into the following groups:

- generic attitude/opinion surveys measuring affect, cognition (ISR) satisfaction, understanding and so on (Cantrell and Benton);

- generic statement-based surveys (12 for Gallup, 7 for Towers Perrin);

- organisation-specific surveys and in-depth interviews (often based on the above templates).

Results can then be analysed by race, gender, age and so on (as in the IES research, for example), nationality (Gallup and Towers Perrin) or broken into branch/site specifics (Gallup) and correlations can be sought between the organisation's or unit's performance, as measured by share prices, sales, staff turnover, customer satisfaction and similar indicators. The Work Foundation

(2005) report proposed a 'company performance indicator' (CPI) to reflect range of performance criteria:

- people – attraction, retention, employee relations for example

- customers and markets

- shareholders

- innovation – including technology, creativity and responsiveness

- stakeholders.

Returning to the assessment of employee engagement itself, rather than its impact, each research organisation tends to have its own dimensions, model, factors or other dimensions to measure. For example, Cantrell and Benton (2005) measure the following five characteristics of employees:

- satisfaction

- understanding

- contribution

- alignment

- retention.

These determine the engagement levels overall, but a more detailed analysis of their statistics led to a ten-point guide to influencing engagement (see 'Role of Leaders', below). In other words, these dimensions are then set against the company characteristics to identify the forces that make the most differences, usually called 'drivers'.

Drivers

It is not always easy to distinguish between the models or dimensions suggested for data collection and those proposed as driver analysis (that is the identification of the elements, internal or external, which are predictive of engagement and which may then be introduced to low-performing organisations). Once again, each commercial organisation has its own approach. For example, Towers Perrin (2004) clusters its findings into three categories (see Figure 12.1):

- leadership and management effectiveness;

- personal effectiveness (employees' need to feel competent, challenged and in control);

- organisational effectiveness (aspects of the company's face to the market and its internal environment).

ISR (2004) collects the elements of engagement under three main headings:

- organisational image (for example, customer approval, high quality products);

TOP 10 ATTRACTION DRIVERS	TOP 10 ENGAGEMENT DRIVERS	TOP 10 RETENTION DRIVERS
1	Work/life balance	Senior management interest in employees	Manager inspires enthusiasm for work
2	Recognition for work	Ability to improve skills	Career advancement opportunities
3	Career advancement opportunities	Senior management demonstrates values	Company reputation as good employer
4	Challenging work	Challenging work	Fair & consistent pay determination
5	Competitive pay	Decision-making authority	Intent to work after retirement in another field
6	Learning/development opportunities	Company reputation as good employer	Decision-making authority
7	Job autonomy	Ability to influence company decisions	Overall work environment
8	Variety of work	Company focus on customer satisfaction	Intent to work after retirement to stay active
9	Pay rises linked to individual performance	Fair & consistent pay determination	Manager provides access to learning opportunities
10	Company reputation as good employer	Overall work environment	Senior management demonstrates values

Source: *2004 European Talent Survey*, Towers Perrin

Proprietary data. Reprinted with permission of Towers Perrin

Source: Towers Perrin (2004), p10.

Figure 12.1   Top drivers of engagement – how employees rate their companies

- leadership (for example, clear management direction, team work);

- people development (for example, effective appraisal, personal development).

IES research (Robinson et al. 2004) found that the key driver was *feeling valued and involved* which meant:

- involved in decision making;

- able to voice ideas and have them valued;

- opportunities to develop the job;

- sense that the organisation is concerned for employees' health and well-being.

This was then turned into the model in Figure 12.2 (overleaf).

The next question was to identify which factors contributed to the sense of feeling valued and involved, which led to the diagnostic tool shown in Figure 12.3.

The Work Foundation report (2005, 20) analysed their research and found that the most engaged companies shared the following characteristics:

- *structure*: unique organisational structure, resulting from geography, size and history, that enables continued success rather than being a specific driver of that success;

- *process*: a higher degree of informality and continued dialogue supported by simple – though not simplistic – processes that allow faster decision making;

- *communication*: openly sharing information between peers and networks of managers that need timely and accurate information in order to get the best job done;

- *leadership*: visible and accessible leadership and management, combined with high expectations from those in decision-making roles.

Source: Robinson et al. 2004 (IES report, p.22)

Figure 12.2   The engagement model

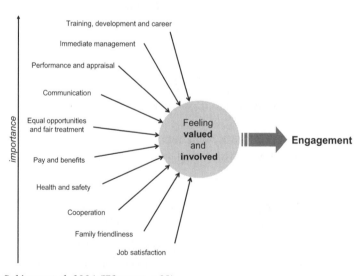

Source: Robinson et al. 2004 (IES report, p.23)

Figure 12.3   Drivers of employee engagement: a diagnostic tool

- *culture and employee relations*: a distrust of the status quo, valuing quality rather than quantity, a focus on the long term and on outcomes; a positive climate characterised – not codified – by pride, innovation and strong interpersonal relations.

Cantrell and Benton (2005) suggested the following drivers determined the level of engagement:

- rewards and recognition
- human capital infrastructure
- learning management
- knowledge management
- performance appraisal
- workplace design
- employee relations
- career development
- recruiting.

Common issues emerge from the approaches listed above, though each has their own approach. Melcrum asked 1000 companies that ran their own driver surveys, which elements emerged as significant; their analysis concluded that the drivers shown in Figure 12.4 appeared in most surveys.

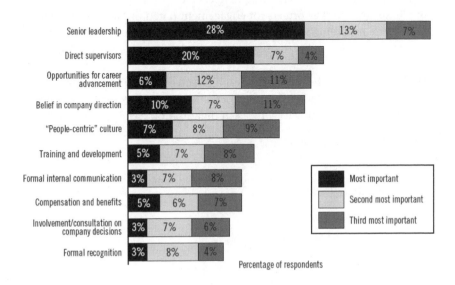

Source: © Melcrum Publishing 2005, p.58

Figure 12.4   Top ten drivers of employee engagement

Problems with survey-dependence and driver analysis

The Melcrum report notes that the number of companies purchasing engagement surveys has risen exponentially since the turn of the century. However, they also found that some managers believed that the survey *was* the engagement process or treated it as an updated satisfaction survey, to be completed once a year and filed away. Even those with a more committed involvement tended to purchase a survey without clarifying their own internal meaning for engagement or appropriate goals for their organisation. Over-reliance on the definitions and priorities established by the survey provider can undermine an organisation's attempts to create a more engaged workforce.

This echoes Welbourne's (2003) criticism of managers who measure instead of 'doing' engagement: 'It's fairly easy to run a point-in-time employee engagement survey and then show scores to managers. When you do this, employee engagement is an 'event' … It's much more difficult to make engagement a way of life in your organisation.'

However, it should also be noted that the Melcrum research showed that some organisations conceptualised employee engagement as a 'vision' rather than a programme of activity and this group tended to do even less than programme subscribers.

This report also identifies a problem with the driver analysis of the type outlined from different companies above, namely that each of the factors is complex and interrelated – and unique to each organisation. Edelman, for example, suggests 40 key drivers for engagement (cited in Melcrum); others put the figure much higher and even those that have reduced the drivers to three or four key 'levers' for change, add multiple subsets to each heading.

Instead of suggesting the answers for each organisation's engagement programme, Melcrum (2005, 84) proposes a more useful process of reflection, the answers to which will vary with each organisation (see Figure 12.5):

- define engagement

- clarify goals

- qualify outcomes

- determine drivers

- measure

- act.

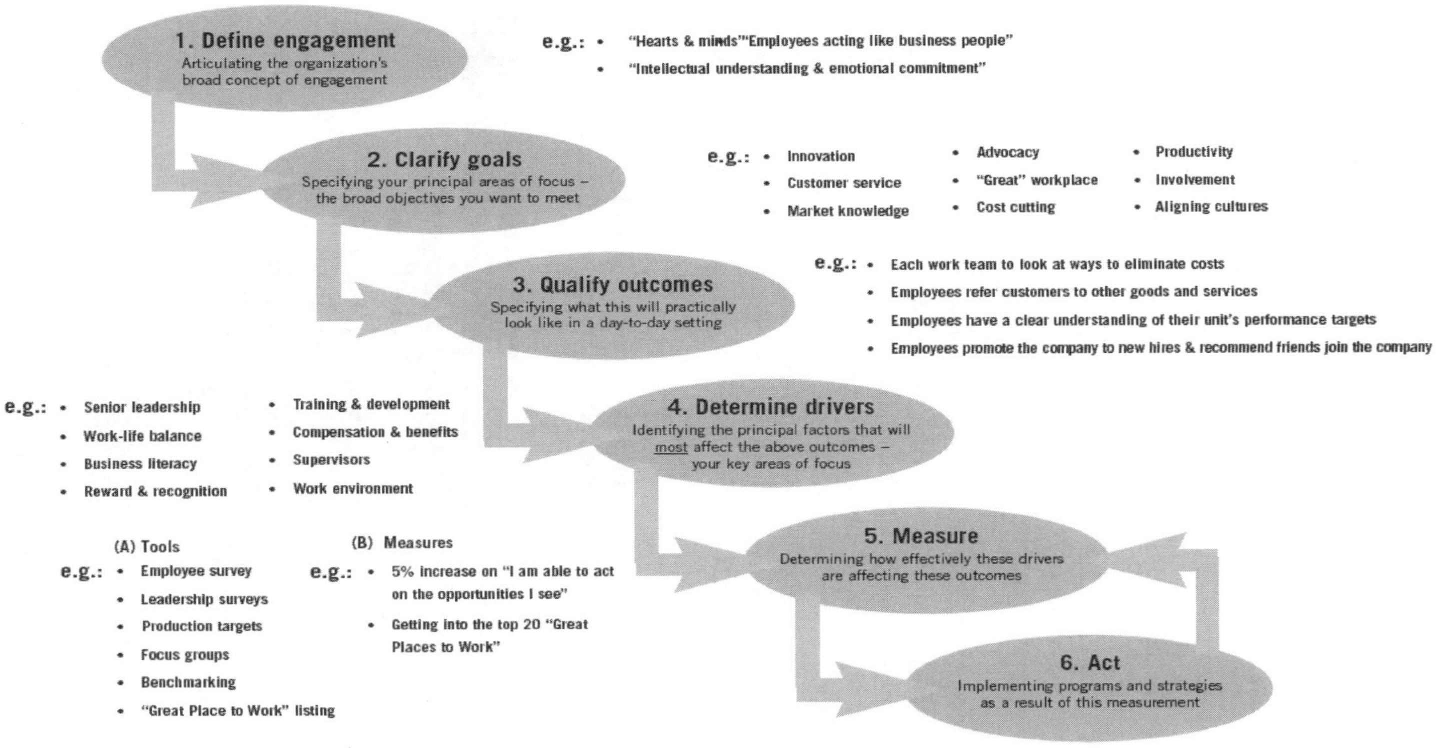

1. Define engagement
Articulating the organization's broad concept of engagement

e.g.: • "Hearts & minds""Employees acting like business people"
• "Intellectual understanding & emotional commitment"

e.g.: • Senior leadership • Training & development
• Work-life balance • Compensation & benefits
• Business literacy • Supervisors
• Reward & recognition • Work environment

2. Clarify goals
Specifying your principal areas of focus – the broad objectives you want to meet

e.g.: • Innovation • Advocacy • Productivity
• Customer service • "Great" workplace • Involvement
• Market knowledge • Cost cutting • Aligning cultures

3. Qualify outcomes
Specifying what this will practically look like in a day-to-day setting

e.g.: • Each work team to look at ways to eliminate costs
• Employees refer customers to other goods and services
• Employees have a clear understanding of their unit's performance targets
• Employees promote the company to new hires & recommend friends join the company

(A) Tools

e.g.: • Employee survey
• Leadership surveys
• Production targets
• Focus groups
• Benchmarking
• "Great Place to Work" listing

(B) Measures

e.g.: • 5% increase on "I am able to act on the opportunities I see"
• Getting into the top 20 "Great Places to Work"

4. Determine drivers
Identifying the principal factors that will most affect the above outcomes – your key areas of focus

5. Measure
Determining how effectively these drivers are affecting these outcomes

6. Act
Implementing programs and strategies as a result of this measurement

Source: © Melcrum Publishing 2005, p.84

Figure 12.5   Strategy process map for clarifying and articulating what engagement means to the organisation

ROLE OF LEADERS

One factor that emerges in almost every driver analysis is the role of leaders, whether that's the CEO or the line manager. This echoes the conclusion of the Gallup research which showed that 'people leave managers, not jobs'.

The Towers Perrin (2004, 11) study showed the relevant drivers of engagement for leadership effectiveness are:

- senior managers have a sincere interest in employee well-being;

- senior managers lead by example in demonstrating company values.

The Work Foundation (2005, 20) study defined the leadership element as: 'visible and accessible leadership and management, combined with high expectations from those in decision-making roles'.

About half of all Melcrum's respondents placed leadership in the top three drivers for engagement, whether or not they conducted driver analysis. Yet 20 per cent also said that their greatest challenge was getting the senior leadership to take ownership of engagement programmes – not a good indicator of leadership, perhaps. The report devotes a whole chapter to the role of senior leaders in engagement workforces, in terms of clear, visionary communication (see also below) and also by living the values they espouse. The key elements by which senior leaders can help build employee engagement are shown in Figure 12.6.

The views of Smythe are represented throughout this book, of course, but it is worth repeating in this context the findings of his research into

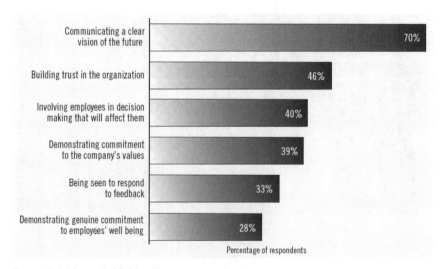

Percentage of respondents

Source: © Melcrum Publishing 2005, p.104

Figure 12.6   Top six most important actions for senior leaders to build employee engagement

leadership styles while a visiting fellow at McKinsey and Company as shown in Figure 12.7.

Taylor (2004 – in Frank) suggests that there are ten essential leadership skills required to retain and engage employees:

- building trust between the team member and the leader;

- building esteem in team members;

- communicating effectively to ... members regarding retention and engagement issues;

- building a climate that is enjoyable and fulfilling;

- being flexible in recognising, understanding and adapting to individual needs and views;

- talent developing and coaching of team members to help them grow, resulting in greater commitment and loyalty to the organisation;

- high performance-building to reinforce high levels of team member performance;

- retention and engagement knowledge that are necessary to build a committed team;

- monitoring retention and engagement team member issues so that pre-emptive action can be taken;

- talent finding.

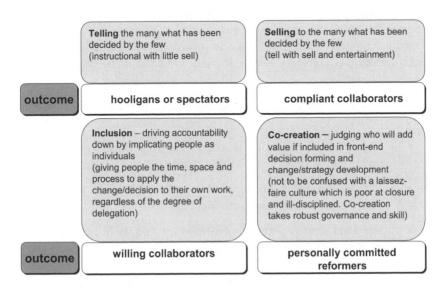

Source: John Smythe and McKinsey & Company

Figure 12.7   Four approaches to engaging people

All the literature and reports surveyed in this chapter agree that, whatever the starting point or motive, the role of leaders – at senior management and line manager level – is crucial to building an engaged workforce.

ROLE OF COMMUNICATORS

Many of the ideas explored above are located in the human resources literature and concentrate on issues like attitudes, motivation, managing people and so on. While several of the key research reports mention communication, few concentrate on the role of communication in building an engaged workforce. It provides one of the ten elements outlined by Taylor (above), for example. However, as the following examples show, it may be one of the keys to success.

The CIPD (2006) certainly believes that the ability of managers to listen to employees is critical: 'Employee commitment and "buy-in" come primarily not from telling but from listening … Two-way communication, both formal and informal, is essential as a form of reality check and a basis for building mutual trust.'

Examples of the effect of poor communication were found in the IABC research report, *Best Practices in Employee Communication: A Study of Global Challenges and Approaches* (Gay et al. 2005). Of 472 organisations surveyed worldwide, only a third reported that their employees were effectively aligned to business strategies and missions and among the reasons cited were inconsistent messages and managers who either didn't understand their roles in employee communications, or lacked the skills or tools to be effective.

Shaffer (2004) argues for creating a high-performance communications system as the foundation for engagement. This must replace the traditional hierarchical models of communication to form an effective link between communication, engagement and performance and should be based on the following principles:

- Create a high-performance communication system (see below for details).

- Select the right performance targets (meaning communication performance driven by business strategy to achieve selected results).

- Narrow the focus for more leverage (don't waste resources on unnecessary engagement activities).

- Fix, track and repeat (involve relevant people, focus on specific problems, monitor and evaluate).

In particular, he suggests that a high-performance communication system can be implemented by the following actions:

- Build a line of sight where people can see the direct link between what they do and how it influences the organisation.

- Increase involvement, which improves information exchanges, gives people a means to influence the organisation and increases ownership.

- Facilitate the sharing of accurate decision making at 'twitch' speed.

- Enhance intrinsic and extrinsic reward and recognition, thereby helping people understand 'what's in it for me?' when they act to improve performance.

The Edelman public relations consultancy has also played a leading role in arguing for the centrality of communication in developing engaged workforces. Their previous Director of Employee Engagement Practice, Christopher Hannegan, is interested in the role of blogs in informal corporate communications (see Edelman and Intelliseek 2005) and has also produced a summary of characteristics of a world-class employee communications function (Hannegan 2006):

- keeps employees focused outward on the customer and the competition rather than inward;

- helps employees understand and believe in where the company is heading, its strategies for getting there and how they can contribute to the mission;

- creates a greater cause for employees to believe in, helps drive the business, not just report on it;

- turns employees into 'backyard-fence spokespeople' for the company and its products;

- provides particularly strong support to employee groups in direct contact with customers (sales force, call centres, customer support and so on);

- partners with other key functions (such as human resources, marketing, strategy, organisational development, operations and business heads) to drive change to help the company achieve its business objectives;

- is the biggest advocate for an integrated communications approach, which includes driving message unity and working closely with media relations, investor relations and advertising.

- Creates rewarding career paths for its practitioners, who work daily in positions offering maximum flexibility;

- matches the sophistication of messaging and communications delivery to audiences, creates communications tools that work for the recipients, not the creators;

- creates a communications culture where communicating is the job of everyone, not just a department;

- measures communications' impact on an ongoing basis in qualitative and quantitative ways.

One of the most interesting reports into employee engagement is the Watson Wyatt (2006) study of the effects of communication on return on investment. This surveyed major North American organisations' performance criteria and then tracked back to survey responses to consider the impact of communications functions on business performance. They found that companies which communicate effectively have a 19.4 per cent higher market premium than companies which do not. Moreover, shareholder returns for organisations with the most effective communication were over 57 per cent higher over the previous five years (2000–2004) than were returns for firms with less effective communication.

The study also concluded with the characteristics of communication in highly effective companies, as evidenced in the research (p.8):

- having a communication programme in place to support an organisational change effort;

- openly communicating with employees about matters that affect them and the reasons behind major decisions;

- linking communication objectives to business objectives;

- sharing business plans and goals with employees;

- engaging senior managers and eliciting their support in the communication process;

- linking pay and benefit programmes to achieving the business strategy;

- having a documented internal communication strategy;

- effectively coordinating internal and external communication;

- regularly providing communication counsel and insight to the CEO and senior management team;

- treating managers as a key audience and sharing information with them in advance.

The engaged employee

So, what does the engaged employee look like? According to the IES (Robinson et al. 2004) research into the NHS, the engaged employee is:

- either male or female;

- more likely to have a minority ethnic background, especially black, Chinese or Asian;

- likely to lose engagement the older they get – until they reach 60, when it rises;

- fit and healthy – employees with disabilities/medical conditions have lower engagement levels, those who have had accidents or injuries at work have significantly less engagement;

- a manager or professional rather than a support worker (though this is not clear-cut);

- a full-time worker;

- free from harassment or abuse at work;

- in possession of a personal development plan.

According to Towers Perrin (2004), an engaged employee agrees with the following statements:

- I understand how my work contributes to the company's overall success.

- I am personally motivated to help the company succeed.

- I am willing to put in a great deal of effort beyond what is normally expected.

- I have a sense of personal accomplishment from my job.

- I would recommend the company to a friend as a good place to work.

- The company inspires me to do my best work.

- The company values are aligned with my personal values.

It is worth remembering, however, that they found only 15 per cent of the Europe-wide sample gave positive responses to these statements (23 per cent of German workers emerge as engaged, compared to 14 per cent of UK employees).

CONCLUSIONS

This chapter has looked at a range of research reports from different sources and analysed them for common themes and issues. The discussion on approaches attempted to group the discussion around a set of dimensions, though these are somewhat loose. A number of different measuring tools and drivers were also examined to compare the instruments used to assess engagement levels and improve employee involvement in organisational goals.

It is clear from this analysis that:

- There is considerable confusion about what engagement means, what it consists of, how it is measured and how it can be raised; this has serious implications for the development of the field.

- Several approaches rely on classic theories from psychology and sociology which are not always examined or acknowledged; other ideas which might be more fruitful are not explored.

- There is little academic literature about employee engagement, though there are older texts on motivation, employee communication and so on; most of the writing comes from commercial research organisations or consultancies.

- The research reports to date show that employee engagement can be shown to be a decisive factor in an organisation's commercial success; there is a huge range of ideas about how this can be achieved.

- Organisational leadership is viewed as an essential element in building and maintaining successful employee engagement, though ownership of the process is also stressed.

- The communication aspects of employee engagement have not been fully explored; much of the writing is by and for HR professionals.

- Social, political and economic contexts are downplayed in some research reports; again, further academic research may bring more of these ideas to bear on the field.

- Likewise, the ethical and philosophical implications of seeking to influence the emotional and psychological states of employees are rarely explored.

In many ways, the above list of omissions is an indication of the novelty of the subject of employee engagement: this is an emerging field. The bedrock of ideas might be older but the current social, political and economic context suggests that it is not one that is likely to disappear. The link between employee engagement and financial performance is convincingly made in most of the research reports covered above – they make the business case that employers will have to address the needs of employees in different and more imaginative ways if they are to survive the coming trends of global ageing, talent shortages and the end of the psychological contract that asked for loyalty in return for job security. It is very interesting that just as the job-for-life is buried, the need for highly motivated and committed workers is revealed. The new contract is going to be much harder to achieve, these reports suggest, but they all agree – employee engagement is already the key to economic success.

REFERENCES

Alderfer, C. (1969), 'An Empirical Test of a New Theory of Human Needs', *Organizational Behavior and Human Performance* 4, 143–175 (cited in Frank et al. 2004).

Antcliff, V., Saundry, R. and Stuart, M. (2005), 'Freelance Worker Networks in Audio-Visual Industries', University of Central Lancashire, Lancashire Business School Working Papers/ESRC No.4 ISSN No. 1742-0628.

Bandura, A. (1971), *Social Learning Theory* (New York: General Learning Press).

Barnes, J. A. (1954), 'Class and Committees in a Norwegian Island Parish', *Human Relations* 7, 39–58 (cited in Antcliff et al. 2005).

Bott, E. (1955), 'Urban Families: Conjugal Roles and Social Networks', *Human Relations* 8, 345–385 (cited in Antcliff et al. 2005).

Bourdieu, P. (1984) *Distinction: A Social Critique of the Judgement of Taste,* London, Routledge. (cited in Antcliff et al. 2005).

Bourdieu, P. and Waquant, L. J. D. (1992), *An Invitation to Reflexive Sociology* (Chicago: University of Chicago Press) (cited in Antcliff et al. 2005).

Buckingham, M. and Coffman, C. (1999), *First, Break All the Rules: What the World's Greatest Managers Do Differently* (Simon & Schuster).

Buckingham, M. and Vosburgh, R. M. (2001), 'The 21st Century Human Resources Function: It's the Talent, Stupid! Identifying and Developing Talent, One Person at a Time, Becomes Our Defining Challenge', *Human Resource Planning* 24:4. www.questia.com/PM.qst?a=o&d=5000948846, accessed 25 April 2006.

Cantrell, S. and Benton, J. M. (2005), 'Harnessing the Power of An Engaged Workforce', *Outlook*. www.accenture.com/outlook.

Castells, M. (2000), *The Rise of the Network Society* (Oxford: Blackwell).

CIPD (2006), *Managing the Psychological Contract*, Factsheet. www.cipd.co.uk, accessed 18 April 2006.

DTI/Work Foundation report (2005), *People, Strategy, Performance, Results from the Second Work and Enterprise Business Survey,* Employment Relations Research Series No 46.

Edelman and Intellseek (2005), *Talking From the Inside Out: The Rise of Employee Bloggers*, Fall 2005. http://edelman.com/image/insights/content/Edelman-Intelliseek%20Employee%20Blogging%20White%20Paper.pdf, accessed 26 February 2007.

Fawkes, J. (2006), 'Public Relations, Propaganda and the Psychology of Persuasion', in Tench and Yeomans.

Festinger, L. (1957), *The Theory of Cognitive Dissonance* (New York: Harper & Row) (cited in Fawkes 2006).

Fishbein, M. and Ajzen, I. (1975), *Belief, Attitude, Intention, and Behavior: An Introduction to Theory and Research* (Reading, MA: Addison-Wesley).

Fishbein, M. and Azjen, I. (1980), 'Predicting and Understanding Consumer Behavior: Attitude-behavior Correspondence' in I. Azjen, I. and M. Fishbein (eds), *Understanding Attitudes and Predicting Social Behavior* (New Jersey: Prentice-Hall) (cited in Fawkes 2006).

Frank, F. D. (2004), 'Introduction to the Special Issue on Employee Retention and Engagement', *Human Resource Planning* 27:3, 11. www.questia.com/

PM.qst?a=o&d=5007552241, accessed.25 April 2006.

Frank, F. D., Finnegan, R.P. and Taylor, C. R. (2004), 'The Race for Talent: Retaining and Engaging Workers in the 21st Century', *Human Resource Planning* 27:3. www.questia.com/PM.qst?a=o&d=5007552247, accessed 25 April 2006.

Gay, C., Mahony, M. and Graves, J. (2005), *Best Practices in Employee Communication: A Study of Global Challenges and Approaches* (IABC). http://news.iabc.com/index.php?s=white_papers&item=42, summary accessed 5 April 2006.

Goffman, E. (1959), *The Presentation of Self in Everyday Life* (London: Penguin Books) (cited in Yeomans 2005).

Gubman, E. (2004), 'From Engagement to Passion for Work: The Search for the Missing Person', *Human Resource Planning* 27:3. www.questia.com/PM.qst?a=o&d=5007579546, accessed 25 April 2006.

Guest, D. E. and Conway, N. (2002), *Pressure at Work and the Psychological Framework* (London: CIPD) (cited in Yeomans 2006).

Hannegan, C. (2006), 'Ten Characteristics of World Class Communicators'. www.edelman.com/speak_up/empeng, accessed 5 April 2006.

Harding, S. (date not known), 'Building an Engaged Workforce', *European Quality* 10:2, 40–49.

Hertzberg, F. (1966), *Work and the Nature of Man* (Cleveland: World Publishing) (cited in Frank et al. 2005).

Hochschild, A. R. (2003), *The Managed Heart: Commercialization of Human Feeling,* 2nd Edition (Berkeley, CA: University of California Press) (cited in Yeomans 2005).

Hofstede G. H. (1991), *Cultures and Organisations* (New York: McGraw-Hill) (cited in Yeomans 2006).

Howard. P. and Howard, J. (2001), *The Owner's Manual for Personality at Work* (Austin, Texas: Bard Press) (cited in Gubman 2004).

Hudson Research (2004). 'One-Third of U.S. Employees Dissatisfied with Their Bosses', 31 March. (cited in Frank et al.)

ISR (International Survey Research) (2005), *Creating Competitive Advantage from Your Employees,* White Paper. www.isrinsight.com/pdf/insight/Engagement%20White%20Paper-US%20Singles.pdf, accessed 1 February 2007.

Jamrog, J. (2004), 'The Perfect Storm: The Future of Retention and Engagement', *Human Resource Planning* 27:3. www.questia.com/PM.qst?a=o&d=5007552251, accessed 25 April 2006.

Kowalski, B. (2002), 'The Engagement Gap: A Growing Crisis for Training and Development', *HR Voice* 3 December 2002. www.workindex.com, accessed 11 April 2006.

Lesser, E. and Prusak, L. (eds) (2004), *Creating Value with Knowledge: Insights from the IBM Institute for Business Value* (New York: Oxford University Press). www.questia.com/PM.qst?a=o&d=103180028, accessed 25 April 2006.

Markus, L H., Cooper-Thomas, H. D. and Allpress, K. N. (2005), 'Confounded by Competencies? An Evaluation of the Evolution and Use of Competency Models', *New Zealand Journal of Psychology* 34:2. www.questia.com/PM.qst?a=o&d=5012083525, accessed 25 April 2006.

Maslow, A. (1943), 'A Theory of Human Motivation,' *Psychological Review* 50, 370–396.

McCrae, R. and Costa, P. Jr. (2002), *Personality in Adulthood, Second Edition: A Five-Factor Theory Perspective* (New York: Guilford) (cited in Gubman 2004).

McGregor, D. (1960), *The Human Side of Enterprise* (McGraw-Hill) (cited in Frank et al. 2004).

Melcrum (2005), *Employee Engagement; How to Build a High-Performance Workforce* (Melcrum Publishing).

Quirke, B. (2002), *Making the Connections: Using Internal Communication to Turn Strategy into Action* (Aldershot: Gower) (cited in Yeomans 2006).

Robinson, D., Perryman, S., Hayday, S. (2004), *The Drivers of Employee Engagement* (Brighton, Sussex: IES Research report).

Rosenberg, M. J. and Hovland, C. I. (1960), 'Cognitive, Affective and Behavioral Components of Attitudes', in C. I. Hovland and M. J. Rosenburg (eds) *Attitude, Organization and Change* (Yale University Press).

Shaffer, J. (2004), 'Measurable Payoff: How Employee Engagement Can Boost Performance and Profits', *Communication World* July–August. www.findarticles.com, accessed 5 April 2006.

Smythe, J. (2005), 'The Democratisation of Strategy and Change: Headlines From a Recent Study into Employee Engagement', *Communication World* March–April. www.findarticles.com, accessed 5 April 2006.

Taylor, C. (2004), 'Retention Leadership', *T+D Magazine* 58:3 (Alexandria: ASTD Press) (cited in Frank et al. 2004).

Tench, R. and Yeomans, L. (2006), *Exploring Public Relations* (London: Pearson Education).

The Corporate Citizenship Company (2003), 'Good Companies, Better Employees'. www.corporate-citizenship.co.uk/publications/HR3_Final.pdf, accessed 31 January 2007 (cited in Melcrum 2005).

The Work Foundation (2001), 'The Ethical Employee Report'. www.theworkfoundation.com, accessed 12 April 2006.

The Work Foundation (2005), 'Cracking the Performance Code: How Firms Succeed'. www.theworkfoundation.com, accessed 12 April 2006.

Thomson K. and Hecker, L. A. (2000), 'The Business Value of Buy-In: How Staff Understanding and Commitment Impact on Brand and Business Performance', in R. J. Varey and B. R. Lewis (eds) *Internal Marketing: Directions for Management* (London: Routledge) (cited in Yeomans 2006).

Towers Perrin (2004) *Reconnecting with Employees – Attracting, Retaining and Engaging Your Workforce* (Towers Perrin study).

Watson Wyatt (2006), *Effective Communication: A Leading Indicator of Financial Performance; 2005/2006,* Communication ROI Study. www.watsonwyattt.com, accessed 11 April 2006.

Welbourne, T. (2003), 'Employee Engagement: Doing it vs Measuring'. www.eepulse.com/documents/pdfs/HR.com-9-8-03.pdf, article from www.HR.com, accessed 20 April 2006.

Yeomans, L. (2005) 'Emotion, Emotional Labour and Public Relations Executives: An Exploration', conference paper presented at Alan Rawel/CIPR Academic Conference, Lincoln UK, March 2005.

Yeomans, L. (2006), 'Internal Communication', in Tench, R. and Yeomans, L.

Index